THE
SAND CREEK
MASSACRE

"Sand Creek, 1864," a wood cut, by Edwina T. Cundall.
Reproduced courtesy of the artist.

THE
Sand Creek
MASSACRE

BY STAN HOIG

UNIVERSITY OF OKLAHOMA PRESS : NORMAN

BY Stan Hoig
Humor of the American Cowboy
(Caldwell, Idaho, 1958)

The Sand Creek Massacre
(Norman, 1961)

The Peace Chiefs of the Cheyennes
(Norman, 1980)

Library of Congress Catalog Card Number: 61–15141

ISBN: 0–8061–1147–X

9   10   11   12   13   14   15   16   17   18   19   20

To a literary saddlemate,
Brent Ashabranner

FOREWORD

THE SAND CREEK MASSACRE—sometimes called the Battle of
Sand Creek by those who would imply it was not a massacre,
or the Chivington Massacre by those who would emphasize
the responsibility of Colonel John M. Chivington—is one of
our most controversial Indian conflicts. For very nearly a full
century, the complete story of the massacre has remained un-
chronicled, largely because of the enormous prejudices which
surround the matter. Even today the site is dedicated by a
compromising historical marker which reads: "Sand Creek
'Battle' or 'Massacre.'"

The subject of army and Congressional investigations and
inquiries, a matter of vigorous newspaper debates, the object
of much oratory and writing extremely biased in both directions, the event itself rife with bitter conflict between the

men who were involved, the Sand Creek Massacre very likely will never be completely resolved.

Undertaken by citizen and military troops enlisted from Colorado Territory, the massacre was, in execution, a local matter. By all available evidence Chivington undertook the Indian expedition on his own, though acting under the vague orders of the preoccupied General Curtis, who was ill informed on the Indian situation. The attack on the Sand Creek Indians, thereby, did not reflect official government policy or plan, although the same counter philosophies of punitive action versus pacification permeated the history of government dealings with the Plains Indians.

The ramifications of the massacre, however, extended far beyond the politics and borders of Colorado Territory. At Sand Creek the era of the Indian trader in Colorado came to a conclusive end, and the dominance of the Cheyennes and Arapahoes to the land east of the mountains was broken. But of greatest importance, the Sand Creek Massacre, probably more than any other Indian conflict, set the stage for the years of bloody battle with the Plains tribes after the Civil War. In the years to follow, it would remain with the Indian as the most potent symbol of white-man treachery.

Those who wish to defend Chivington point to the depredations and murders committed by the Cheyennes and Arapahoes prior to the massacre. These crimes are here acknowledged for the period between the killing of Lean Bear on May 16, 1864, and the meeting on the Smoky Hill on September 10, 1864, during which time the Cheyennes and Arapahoes were at war. Prior to the attacks by Dunn, Downing, and Eayre on Cheyenne villages and the death of Lean Bear, however, it is difficult to substantiate any major crimes committed in Colorado Territory by these tribes.

This book attempts merely to trace the action and events surrounding the Sand Creek Massacre and, by so doing, to fix responsibility, leaving the personal motivations to be questioned by others. It does not attempt to argue with the many misstatements, uses of faulty authority, and invalid arguments which have been made in support of both sides of the Sand Creek debate. If this book reduces the number of such errors, then some purpose will have been served.

The large body of this material rests solidly upon authoritative foundation. Interpretation of some of the incidents which involved conflicting testimony relies upon supporting evidence, where possible, or upon logic where no further support was available.

This writer wishes to acknowledge the full co-operation and assistance of the Colorado State Historical Society, the Denver Public Library, the Houston Public Library, the Kansas State Historical Society, the University of Texas Library, Fondren Library of Rice University, the Library of Congress, the Smithsonian Institution, the National Archives, with personal thanks to the following individuals whose help was willing and generous: Mrs. Agnes Wright Spring, Colorado state historian; Mrs. Laura Ally Ekstrom, assistant librarian, Colorado State Historical Society; Mrs. Alys Freeze, head, Western History Department, Denver Public Library; Mr. Robert W. Richmond, archivist, Kansas State Historical Society; and Mr. Benton H. Wilcox, Wisconsin State Historical Society. My thanks also to Mr. Bob McGrath, Lamar, Colorado, for showing me around the ruins of Fort Lyon and Bent's Fort; to Mr. Michael Straight of Alexandria, Virginia, who contributed some im-

portant research information; and to my wife for her enthu-
siasm and help in the research, note taking, and preparation
of this book.

STAN HOIG

Houston, Texas

CONTENTS

ILLUSTRATIONS

THE
SAND CREEK
MASSACRE

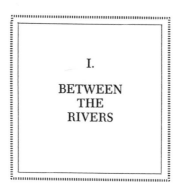

I.

BETWEEN
THE
RIVERS

Daybreak of November 29, 1864, swelled over the land's edge in southeastern Colorado Territory and moved westward across the mesquite-spotted sand hills, revealing the village of Black Kettle's Cheyennes nestled in a bend of the dry-bedded Sand Creek. Here a small range of bluffs halted the southerly meandering of the creek, forcing it to an easterly course for nearly a mile before it once again turned southward. A few cottonwood and willow, bare of foliage, marked the bend, and near them, below the Cheyennes, were camped eight lodges of Arapahoes under Chief Left Hand. On the flat land north of the river, east of the encampment, a horse herd grazed indolently while another was scattered over the backside of the bluffs to the south.

The cone-shaped lodges, more than one hundred of them,

gleamed white and clean in the early light. Only a few trails of smoke rose from the village, hardly swirling in the frozen air of morning. A tightly-blanketed Indian woman, out to gather firewood, saw a strange cloud of dust to the south along the river and hurried to report it. At first the cloud was thought to mean a buffalo herd; then someone said the soldiers were coming. Even as the village jerked to life, the crisp silence of the winter's sunrise was split by the slap of gunfire and the shrill yelping of cavalry troops galloping around the sand bluffs and across the creek. Thus began the Sand Creek Massacre.

For more than forty years the country between the Platte and the Arkansas rivers, from central Kansas to the Rocky Mountains, had been the domain of the Southern Cheyenne and Arapaho Indians. South of the Arkansas the arrogant and powerful Kiowas and Comanches held the broken lands of the Staked Plains. North of the Platte ranged the angry Sioux. But between the rivers the Cheyennes ruled, a proud and warlike people who shared the vacuous prairies with their confederate tribe, the less noble but equally warlike Arapahoes. Here bands of the two tribes wandered nomadically over the naked hills, camped their villages along the wide-bottomed streams, hunted buffalo, and made war for war upon enemy tribes.

It was early in the nineteenth century that the Cheyenne and Arapaho tribes split, and a large portion of them drifted to the region south of the Platte, held there by the great buffalo herds, by the trading posts of the fur traders, by the commerce along the Arkansas wagon route, and by the government annuities issued at Atkinson and other forts. In 1851 the treaty of Fort Laramie legally defined the country be-

4

tween the rivers as the domain of the Cheyennes and Arapahoes and cemented the peaceful relations between the Indians and the whites who migrated across their land.

The Cheyennes and Arapahoes had traditionally been friendly to the white man, and it wasn't until 1856 that an incident occurred between troops at Fort Laramie and a band of Northern Cheyennes, creating the first outbreak of hostilities by the tribes. This trouble was resolved the following year when Colonel E. V. "Old Bull" Sumner took to the field and routed a large body of Cheyenne warriors on the Republican River with a saber charge, later confiscating their annuity goods at Bent's New Fort on the Arkansas.

In 1858 the gold rush to the Pikes Peak and South Platte region ignited a stampede of whites across the plains equivalent to that of the California gold rush of 1849. But this time the whites did not pass on into the mountains. Instead, they built towns and settled down to stay.

The Indians continued their friendly acceptance of the whites who passed through their hunting grounds, content to exact what tolls they could for the passage.[1] In newly founded, rapidly growing Denver City, Indians were seen daily on the streets or in camp near the town. One of the most noted of the Indian visitors was the Arapaho Chief Little Raven, who had a talk with the people of Denver and "pledged his word for the preservation of peace and law and order by his people."[2]

[1] LeRoy R. Hafen (ed.), *Pike's Peak Gold Rush Guidebooks of 1859*, 326.

[2] The meeting was postponed for a day when the interpreter, Antoine de Bray, fell off the chair next to Little Raven from the effects of too much alcohol. Little Raven was described as a "very sensible and friendly disposed man" who "handles knife and fork and smokes his cigars like a white man." LeRoy R. Hafen (ed.), *Colorado Gold Rush—Contemporary Letters and Reports 1858–1859*, 349, 357, 363–64.

5

Little Raven explained that he liked the white men and was glad to see them getting gold, reminding them, however, that the land belonged to the Indians. He hoped they would not say anything bad to his people who were scattered over the prairie and that they would not stay around too long.[3]

Following this conference, the Indians visited Denver in numbers and associated with the whites on equal terms. Such familiarity, as Tom Fitzpatrick, their first agent, had strongly opposed, was bound to lead to trouble. On April 14, 1860, a group of white men, reportedly led by Big Phil the Cannibal, visited an Arapaho camp near the town while the men were gone and raped some of the women.[4] When they left, they stole three of the Indians' mules. Youthful Chief Left Hand threatened reprisal but was talked out of it by old Jim Beckwith, who wrote a letter to the *Rocky Mountain News* denouncing the Denver "drunken devils and bummers," warning readers, "The Indians are as keenly sensible to acts of injustice as they are tenacious of revenge."[5] This and other mis-

[3] Nolie Mumey, *History of the Early Settlements of Denver* (1859–1860), 134–35.

[4] James H. Baker and LeRoy R. Hafen (eds.), *History of Colorado,* I, 380.

[5] *Rocky Mountain News* (Denver, April 18, 1860). James P. Beckwith (Beckwourth) was famous in the West as early as 1856 when his biography was written by T. D. Bonner. A mulatto born in Virginia, Beckwith came west in the early 1820's and spent a good deal of time among the Crow Indians, rising to the status of a chief. He later served with the army in Florida and spent some time as a trapper and fur trader in Colorado, New Mexico, and California. At one time he operated a saloon in Santa Fe, and was around Fort Pueblo on the Arkansas in the 1840's. In November of 1859, Beckwith returned to Denver from St. Louis in the employ of A. P. Vásquez and Company. He became a part of the early years of Denver. In 1865 he was sixty-nine years of age and still hale and hearty. LeRoy R. Hafen, "The Last Years of James P. Beckwourth," *The Colorado Magazine,* Vol. V (1928), 134–39.

conduct by the whites greatly disturbed the Indians, who were concerned already by the number of whites crowding in on their lands.

William Bent,[6] whose forts on the Arkansas had long been the citadels of the untamed country between the Missouri River and the Rockies, had foreseen the great dangers involved. As Cheyenne and Arapaho agent in 1859, he wrote:

> The concourse of whites is therefore constantly swelling, and incapable of control or restraint by the government. This suggests the policy of promptly rescuing the Indians, and withdrawing them from contact with the whites. . . . These numerous and warlike Indians, pressed upon all around by the Texans, by the settlers of the gold region, by the advancing people of Kansas, and from the Platte, are already compressed into a small circle of territory, destitute of food, and itself bisected athwart by a constantly marching line of emigrants. A

[6] William Bent came to the Arkansas country with his three brothers in the late 1820's, and in the early 1830's he and St. Vrain opened the famous post on the Arkansas near present-day La Junta, Colorado. In 1837 he married a Cheyenne Indian woman, Owl Woman, and the next year their first child was born—a girl, named Mary. During the following years other children arrived: three sons who were named for Bent's brothers, Robert, George, and Charles, and another daughter, Julia. When Owl Woman died, Bent took her sister, Yellow Woman, as his wife. In 1849, disgusted with the War Department for not offering a suitable price for his fort at the mouth of the Purgatoire, Bent destroyed it and moved downstream to the Big Timbers, a few miles west of present-day Lamar, Colorado, where in 1853 he began construction of a new fort, smaller but built of stone rather than sod. This same year Bent took his three oldest children—Mary, Robert, and George—to Westport and turned them over to a friend who became their guardian for a time. Charles followed them later, but Julia remained on the Arkansas, where she married the half-blood product of mountain man Bill Guerrier, Edmund Guerrier, who had been educated at St. Mary's Mission in Kansas. During these years the Cheyennes and Arapahoes leaned heavily on Bent's advice and counsel, and the unnatural peace they kept with the whites owed much to the "Little White Man."

7

desperate war of starvation and extinction is therefore imminent and inevitable, unless prompt measures shall prevent it.[7]

Commissioner of Indian Affairs A. B. Greenwood reported
that "There is no alternative to providing for them in this
manner but to exterminate them, which the dictates of justice
and humanity alike forbid."[8] He recommended new treaties
with the Cheyennes and Arapahoes, and in 1860, Congress
appropriated $35,000 for the holding of a council with those
tribes on the Upper Arkansas.

In August of that year, Commissioner Greenwood himself
left Washington for Bent's New Fort with a party consisting
of his son, a nephew, a brother-in-law, the son of Secretary
of the Interior Thompson, and several private friends. He also
hired two Delaware Indians as escorts at five dollars a day,
"there being nothing to guide them, except the river and the
broad wagon road extending all the way."[9] Greenwood arrived at the fort on September 8, followed by thirteen wagonloads of trinkets and goods for treating with the Indians.[10]

The War Department, in the meantime, had decided to

[7] *Annual Report* of the Commissioner of Indian Affairs, 1859, p. 507.

Bent obviously had help in writing this letter, probably from the superintendent of Indian affairs in St. Louis. In more his own style, Bent wrote
in 1859, "The Cheyans and Arrapahos have took my advice to them last
Winter and this last Spring. I am proud to say they have behaved themselves
exceedingly well. . . . Theair will be no troble settling them down and start
farming. They tell me they . . . have passed theair laws amongst themselves
that they will do anything I may advize. It is a pitty that the Department
can't send Some farming implements and other necessarys this fall Sow as
they could commence farming this Coming Spring. . . . you Must excuse my
bad Spelling as I have bin so long in the Wild Waste I have almost forgotten
how to Spell." David Lavender, *Bent's Fort*, 341–42.

[8] *Annual Report* of the Commissioner of Indian Affairs, 1859, p. 385.

[9] *The Western Mountaineer*, Golden, Colo., October 4, 1860, p. 6.

[10] *Annual Report* of the Commissioner of Indian Affairs, 1860, pp. 248,
452; *Western Mountaineer*, September 20, 1860.

build an army post at the site of Bent's New Fort, which had been purchased by the government. The post was to be called Fort Wise, in honor of the governor of Virginia. Major John Sedgwick, who had been pursuing the marauding Kiowas and Comanches along the Arkansas and had just returned to the Pawnee Fork from Bent's Fort, was ordered back up the river for the purpose of building the army post and assisting in the treaty with the Indians.[11]

A site was selected up the river a mile from Bent's place, and 350 troops of First Cavalry and Tenth Infantry began construction of Fort Wise early in September.[12] The wagon train carrying the tools and building supplies having been delayed by the cost-conscious army, the soldiers improvised their own implements, cutting long cottonwood poles to use as crowbars for prying up the huge ledge stones which jutted from the surrounding bluffs in abundance. Axes were used to quarry the rock, and trowels for the masonry were fashioned from old stovepipe and wheel iron.

All the buildings of the new post were made of stone, with flat, dirt-covered roofs, dirt floors, and windows made of beef hides stretched on stick frames. A steady stream of wagons—165 six-mule loads of stone each day—made their way from the post to the bluffs on the north, while soldiers worked feverishly at unloading rock and plastering it into walls to outspeed the cold weather that was due to set in soon.

[11] *Correspondence of John Sedgwick Major General,* II, 18. On the road behind Sedgwick was Lieutenant J. E. B. Stuart, accompanied by Bent's oldest son, Robert, returning from school in Missouri.

[12] *Correspondence of John Sedgwick,* 19; J. E. B. Stuart Diary (Microfilm, Kansas State Historical Society); *The Western Mountaineer,* September 20, 1860, pp. 6–7, October 4, 1860, p. 6; *Rocky Mountain News,* October 30, 1860, p. 2; Leavenworth *Daily Times,* October 23, 1860.

A large group of Arapahoes had preceded Sedgwick and encamped along the Arkansas Valley, filling the bottom with lodges, while droves of ponies, mules, and oxen grazed indolently on the prairie along the river. Indians walked about the area slowly and stately, covered, as a reporter put it, "with blankets, leggings, paint, lice and dirt."[13]

Bent's Fort, perched on a stone bluff at the river's edge below the new post, had taken on the atmosphere of a thriving frontier community. Indians, Mexicans, half-bloods of all varieties, men from the plains and mountains, tenderfeet from the East rode in and out of the fort. William Bent was there, joined by his friend Albert G. Boone. Frontiersmen like John Hatcher, Charlie Autobees, and John Smith were also present, impressing the "civilized world" with a wide variety of languages and dialects. An added attraction was provided by the appearance of a young man named Mark Ralfe, who had recently been speared in the back three times, shot in three other places, scalped, and left for dead by a band of Kiowas. Ralfe managed to make it the thirty-five miles to the fort, where he bid fair to recover, though now without hair except for a small lock above each ear.[14]

13 *The Western Mountaineer,* October 4, 1860, p. 6.

14 *Daily Times,* October 23, 1860.

Captain Lambert Wolf, serving with Sedgwick's command, made these entries concerning Ralfe in his diary: "August 8 . . . He (Bent) sent an express after us, who was overtaken 25 miles from the Fort, shot, scalped, and left for dead, but some friendly Cheyennes found him and took him back to the fort.

"August 29, I visited Bent's Fort and saw his scalped messenger. . . . His hair was all gone, less a small strip behind his right ear. The tomahawk wound on the top of his head was nearly healed up, a thin guazy skin had grown over the scalp part. . . ." George A. Root (ed.), "Extracts from Diary of Captain Lambert Wolf," *The Kansas State Historical Quarterly,* Vol. I (1931–32), 209–10.

Thus far only the Arapahoes had shown. A Captain Potts had been sent out in advance by Greenwood for the purpose of getting the Indians together. Arriving at the fort, he sent out messengers to the Indians, but the ones sent to the Cheyenne camp, supposedly 250 miles away, were not heard from and others were sent out. Then, when a band of Kiowas threatened to attack the fort, Potts left for a healthier climate.

A band of Comanches with about fifty lodges had encamped some twenty-five miles above Bent's, and three of the chiefs, known as Old Woman, Black Bird, and Strong Arm, came in for an interview with Greenwood. After ceremoniously shaking hands with the "Great Captain" and embracing him with a couple of ardent hugs, the head chief opened his parley with, "Christ is over us, and we should be good children."[15] Greenwood, however, pointed out that the Comanches had not been very good children with their constant attacks along the road and refused to issue them the goods they desired.

Medals bearing the likeness of "Old Functionary," President Buchanan, were presented to Arapaho Chiefs Little Raven and Storm. Little Raven lost his and was unconsolable, offering ten horses as a reward for its recovery. A couple of frontier wags ceremoniously gave two Arapaho bucks medals of their own—political campaign buttons, one for Douglas and one for Lincoln—which they wore about with lofty pride.[16]

Left Hand, who had been out on a raid against the Pawnees with forty of his braves, returned to the fort bearing a "scalp with no hair on it," disgusted with an enemy who was cowardly enough to shave his head without leaving a scalp lock. The lone scalp, however, provided an excuse for a victory

[15] *Daily Times,* October 23, 1860.
[16] *The Western Mountaineer,* October 4, 1860, p. 6.

dance, which rendered complete the carnival of frontier life.[17]

Since the Cheyennes and Arapahoes had been treated together in the treaty of Fort Laramie, it was desired to do so again. Finally toward the middle of September Cheyenne Chiefs Black Kettle and White Antelope, with several of their subchiefs, arrived at the fort. Their bands, they said, could not reach the fort in less than twenty days, but Greenwood, who had a treaty-making date with the Kaws in Kansas, could not wait for them. He hurriedly called the Cheyenne and Arapaho chiefs together for a council, issuing them a third of the treaty goods—blankets, shirts, scissors, knives, camp kettles, flour, bacon, sugar, coffee, and tobacco—promising to distribute the remainder of the gifts when the chiefs had signed a treaty.[18]

An agreement seemed difficult to reach. Bent insisted that, as the Indians wished, the whole Fontaine-qui-bouille River region should be reserved for the Cheyennes, while the Arapahoes wanted all of the Arkansas River country above Bent's Fort. "Of course," a correspondent wrote, "settlers would object; and if any arrangement is made, the Indians will probably be put over on the Republican, or in some other locality where they will not interfere with 'our manifest destiny.' "[19]

The chiefs expressed their willingness to quit a wild life and go to farming if the government would send out farmers to show them how to work. Frontiersmen at the fort, however, doubted seriously that the tribes, especially the young men, were actually ready to settle down to an agricultural life, despite, as one expressed it, some signs that the Indians were

[17] *Ibid.*
[18] *Daily Times,* October 23, 1860.
[19] *The Western Mountaineer,* September 20, 1860, pp. 6–7.

"fast becoming civilized. They get drunk as readily as white men and swear with great distinctiveness."[20]

Greenwood expressed the satisfaction of their great father that the Cheyennes and Arapahoes had remained peaceful in the midst of other hostile tribes. The chiefs stated in return that they were greatly pleased that their white father had heard of their good conduct and that they wished to conform to the desires of the government in every way possible. Greenwood then showed them a diagram of the country assigned to them under the treaty of 1851 ". . . which they seemed to understand perfectly, and were enabled, without difficulty, to give each initial point. In fact, they exhibited a degree of intelligence seldom to be found among tribes, where no effort has heretofore been made to civilize them."[21]

The Commissioner made verbal agreements with the Arapahoes, promising to send out the proper documents as soon as he reached Washington. Black Kettle and White Antelope were willing to accept Greenwood's propositions for settling the tribe on a reserve, but refused to bind their people until the question had been put to a vote of all their braves. They would make no commitments until the papers had arrived.

On September 20, Greenwood departed, placing F. B. Culver in charge of the treaty goods. William Bent resigned his office of Indian agent, and in replacement the Indians requested "that good man with a grey beard"—Colonel Boone.[22]

[20] *Ibid.* October 4, 1860, p. 6.

[21] *Annual Report* of the Commissioner of Indian Affairs, 1860, pp. 452–53.

[22] *The Western Mountaineer*, October 4, 1860, p. 6. Albert G. Boone was a grandson of Daniel Boone. Born in St. Charles, Missouri, in 1806, he first came to the Rocky Mountains in 1826 as a bookkeeper with an Ashley furtrading expedition. For several years he was a merchant at Westport, Missouri, and was active on the proslavery side during the Kansas struggle. He came to Denver in 1860 and opened a store, but upon his appointment as

Supported by Bent's recommendation, Boone was appointed to the position by Buchanan.

It was February of 1861 before Boone returned from Washington with the official papers for the Indians to sign and consumate the treaty of Fort Wise. By it the Indians agreed to relinquish their claims to all lands except a gameless, arid section of southeastern Colorado Territory, which was to serve as a reservation for them. In return the United States agreed to protect the Indians on the reservation, to pay them the sum of $30,000 a year for fifteen years ($15,000 to each tribe), to purchase stock and agricultural implements, to build storehouses, to fence land, and to break the soil for the Indians, the expense coming out of the $30,000. In addition, the government agreed to provide the Indians with a sawmill, one or more mechanic shops, dwelling houses, interpreters, millers, farmers, and mechanics to help them out, at a cost not to exceed $5,000 for the next five years. Each Indian was to have forty acres of land, with timber and water where possible.[23]

The influence of Denver business interests in the affair is apparent in Article 11 of the treaty, later struck out by the Senate, which would have allowed Colorado businessmen to enter city and town lots on the reservation at $1.25 an acre. A postscript to the treaty awarded half-bloods Robert Bent and Jack Smith, son of Interpreter John Smith,[24] each 640 acres of choice land along the Arkansas Valley.

Indian agent he moved to the Arkansas and established Booneville, also operating a store in nearby Pueblo. He was later Indian agent for the Kiowas and Comanches in Indian Territory, dying in Denver in 1884.

[23] C. J. Kappler (ed.), *Indian Affairs*, II, 807–11.

[24] No white man, not even William Bent, knew the Cheyennes better than did hawk-faced John Simpson Smith. He left St. Louis in 1830 to wed him-

The treaty was signed by Little Raven, Storm, Shave-Head, and Big Mouth for the Arapahoes, and for the Cheyennes by Black Kettle, White Antelope, Lean Bear, Little Wolf, Tall Bear, and Left Hand (signing with the Cheyennes) on February 18, 1861.

During the spring of 1861 the Indians were quiet along the Arkansas, preparing for the summer buffalo hunt. William Gilpin, governor and superintendent of Indian affairs for Colorado Territory, wrote on June 19, 1861, that Agent Boone had received and stored at Fort Wise the goods forwarded for

self to the great freedom of the West. After eight years trapping in the mountains, living off and on with the Blackfeet and the Sioux, Smith drifted southward in 1838 to the Arkansas and began trading activities for William Bent. During this time he learned the Cheyenne language, took up with a Cheyenne Indian woman, and became a member of the tribe, eventually winning himself a respected place in council as a Cheyenne subchief. The Indians knew him as "Blackfeet" or "Gray Blanket." Smith was wintering along the Arkansas in 1846–47 when young Lewis Garrard wandered west for some adventure, met Smith, and joined him for the winter with the Cheyennes. Garrard later wrote in his book, *Wah-to-yah and the Taos Trail,* in which Smith played a leading role:

"He became such an adept in the knowledge of the Cheyenne tongue, and such a favorite with the tribe, that his services as trader were now quite invaluable to his employers. Possessed of a retentive memory, he still spoke the dialects of the three nations just named [Blackfoot, Sioux, and Cheyenne]: and, in addition, French like a native, Spanish very well, and his mother tongue. Though subject to privations of a severe nature, he thought it 'better to reign in hell than serve in heaven' and nothing could persuade him to lead a different life." Ralph P. Bieber (ed.) *Wah-to-yah and the Taos Trail,* 114–17.

Garrard also became acquainted with Smith's young half-blood son, Jack, then three or four years of age, "plainly showing in his complexion and features, the mingling of American and Indian blood." *Ibid.,* 95–96.

During the 1840's Smith, along with Kit Carson and some of the other Bent traders, helped to build the first Fort Adobe on the South Canadian River in the Texas Panhandle. In the summer of 1847, Smith commanded Fort Mann on the Santa Fe Trail for a short time, but soon quit and ended up in Santa Fe, where Fitzpatrick hired him as an interpreter for the newly established Upper Platte and Arkansas Indian Agency.

During the years that followed, Smith served as needed as interpreter and

the Cheyenne and Arapaho bands for the current season, but that he had instructed Boone to hold the annuities until fall, knowing that at the setting in of cold weather the Indians would be most destitute.[25]

The summer of 1861 was a dry one, and the country along the Arkansas became parched and dried up with the heat and lack of rain. By September the tribes, suffering badly from hunger, were clamoring for their annuities. Several thousand Indians collected around Fort Wise, and some were threatening the fort, giving the whites ten days to pay their annuities. The commanding officer of the feebly garrisoned post, Captain Elmer Otis, distributed some provisions among the Indians and quieted them down.[26]

In October, Boone was at Fort Wise with an amended version of the Fort Wise treaty, which had been ratified by Congress on August 6, for the Indians to sign. Toward the end of the month the Cheyennes began arriving at the fort, and on

---

was employed in this capacity during the treaty of Fort Laramie council in 1851. He later accompanied Fitzpatrick and a group of chiefs to Washington, D. C., where they visited President Fillmore. Smith left the Arkansas in the 1850's and moved to the South Platte country, where he traded for Elbridge Gerry out of Fort Laramie. As a result, Smith, a "gray-bearded old sinner," was the first white man met by the gold rush group at the mouth of Cherry Creek in 1858. He was a big help to the new arrivals, and assisted the Russell group in building the first log cabin on the site of present-day Denver. For a time "Uncle John" Smith took part in the settlement of the new city in the wilderness. But his encounter with civilization was short-lived, and he was reportedly run out of town for beating his Indian wife with a three-legged creepy because she danced with the miners. He turned up once again on the Arkansas, now with a new Indian wife, and was on hand to interpret during the treaty of Fort Wise in 1860. He is not to be confused with the John W. Smith mentioned by Captain Eugene F. Ware in *The Indian War of 1864.*

25 *Annual Report* of the Commissioner of Indian Affairs, 1861, p. 709.

26 *Rocky Mountain News*, September 9, 1861, p. 2.

October 29, Boone again secured their signatures. On December 5, 1861, President Abraham Lincoln proclaimed the treaty.[27]

The government had answered Bent's plea for a definition of the Indians' rights by reducing their domain to a slight fraction of that given them under the Fort Laramie treaty. The whites in Colorado now legally owned the land they had invaded, bought for them at a price that would never be paid. Before that, the Indians would be driven to war.

[27] Kappler (ed.) *Indian Affairs*, II, 807–11.

II.

INDIAN
AFFAIRS
1863

IN THE SPRING OF 1861 the clouds of civil war drifted toward the mountains. With the problem of the Indians supposedly solved, Colorado Territory turned to a more pressing question —Union or secession? The Southerners in the territory attempted to organize, but the strength of the predominant Northern sympathizers soon became apparent. Under Territorial Governor Gilpin, miners weary of the rough mining camps were mustered into volunteer military regiments and the rebellious Southern leaders drifted off southward to join the Confederate armies.

During the summer of 1861, a Confederate army of Texans began a march from El Paso up the Rio Grande Valley toward Colorado Territory, capturing Albuquerque and then Santa Fe. A call for help went out from the Union forces in New

18

Mexico Territory. It was answered by the Colorado First Regiment of Volunteers who made a hasty and heroic march to Fort Union.

The Coloradans, combined with units of the New Mexico Union forces, met the Texans at La Glorieta Pass east of Santa Fe on March 26, 1862, and advance guards of the two armies fought an inconclusive battle in Apache Canyon. On March 28, Colonel John Slough, Denver lawyer who commanded the Union forces, moved forward to meet the Texans, sending nearly a third of his command over a mountainous route to attack from the Confederates' rear.

The flanking movement was under the command of Major John M. Chivington,[1] who had been in charge of the Union troops during the Apache Canyon fracas and had proved himself a capable leader under fire. While Slough's forces engaged the advancing rebels that morning, Chivington made his circuitous march and suddenly found himself looking down from a mountainous height onto the entire baggage train of the Confederates. After reconnoitering the situation carefully, Chivington sent his troops charging down upon the wagon train and routed the defenders. Eighty-five wagons, all heavily loaded with ammunition, clothing, subsistence, and for-

---

[1] John M. Chivington was born in Ohio in 1821. Taking up the ministry in 1844, he preached in Ohio, Illinois, Missouri, Kansas, and Nebraska prior to his arrival in Denver on May 19, 1860, as presiding elder of the First Methodist Episcopal Church. He immediately began organization of the first Methodist Sunday school in Denver, and traveled to various mining towns to preach. Originally tendered a commission as chaplain of the First Regiment, he refused this and requested a "fighting" commission rather than a "praying" one. He was a man of enormous physique, over six feet in height and around 250 pounds, with a barrel chest and bull neck. One man who knew him described Chivington as the most perfect figure of a man he had ever seen in a uniform.

age, were captured and burned on the spot. An estimated five to six hundred horses and mules were bayoneted to death.

It was nothing less than a *coup de maître* that Chivington's force laid upon the Confederates, destroying any hope for their continued advance and sending them retreating back down the Rio Grande Valley to Texas. The Colorado First Regiment remained in New Mexico for most of 1862, returning that fall to posts along the Platte, to Camp Weld in Denver, and to the Arkansas where Fort Wise was now renamed Fort Lyon, for the first Union general killed in the Civil War, Nathaniel Lyon. Colonel Slough, having resigned his command for not being allowed to further punish the Texans, was replaced in command by Chivington, who was now appointed commanding colonel of the newly created military district of Colorado.

Clearly, if the Indians had wanted a war with the whites, 1862 was the year for it. With most of her military forces drawn to New Mexico, Colorado Territory was virtually defenseless against Indian attack. The Cheyennes and Arapahoes remained at peace, however, and in the fall newly appointed Governor John Evans[2] heaved a sigh of relief and reported to the Commissioner of Indian Affairs, ". . . and now that the War Department has ordered the Colorado troops

---

[2] Gilpin was removed from office for issuing drafts against the government without authorization, and Lincoln appointed John Evans to replace him. Evans was born in Ohio in 1814, studied medicine at Clermont Academy in Pennsylvania, and held a position with the Rush Medical College in Chicago. He was involved in the founding of Northwestern University and assisted in founding Evanston, Illinois, which is named after him. He took an active part in the first Republican Convention in the United States, held at Aurora, Illinois, and supported Lincoln in the 1860 campaign. He was offered the position of governor of the territory of Washington but declined, later accepting the Colorado appointment.

home, and mounted one regiment, giving us ample military protection, we have but little danger to apprehend from Indian hostilities. . . ."[3]

Meanwhile, little had been done toward putting the treaty of Fort Wise into effect. None of the necessary arrangements for the settlement of any of the Indians on the reserve could be made until it was determined specifically what Indians were to have lands allotted to them and until they were enrolled. With the numerous bands of the two tribes wandering at will over the vast plains from Larned to Lyon and from the Arkansas to the Platte, it was impossible to accomplish such an accounting.[4]

Early in 1863 the first Indian trouble began to develop in Colorado Territory. The Utes were raiding in west-central Colorado, and five companies of Colorado First troops were put into the field under Major Edward W. Wynkoop to find and chastise them. One party of Utes had visited Medicine Bow Station near Camp Collins, taken provisions, and stripped two men of their shirts and cravats in the process, but otherwise not harming them. After an extended and empty search for the marauders, Wynkoop returned to Denver.

The Utes and the Cheyennes had been exchanging war blows for years, and war parties of both tribes periodically traveled past the white settlements on their way to the enemy's camp. A Denver pioneer gives a good description of such an incident, "One beautiful Sunday morning, during my first year in Denver [1861], I remember being startled by a most weird and unfamiliar sound, which sent me to the door to learn its source. From there I saw a band of Indians coming

[3] *Annual Report* of the Commissioner of Indian Affairs, 1862, pp. 373–76.
[4] *Ibid.*, p. 375.

up our street, and a minute later thirty or more Cheyennes and Arapahoes passed by, holding aloft on poles five freshly-taken Ute scalps."[5]

Others recalled Utes on their way east to fight the Cheyennes and Arapahoes, the Indians making the trip at least once a year. Agent Colley reported that it was impossible to prevent the Cheyennes from warring on the Utes—" . . . in fact it is a part of their life, being taught it from infancy."[6]

It was on an excusion to Ute country that the Cheyennes had their first trouble with the whites in Colorado Territory. In March of 1863 some citizens of Weld County near the mouth of the Cache la Poudre River complained that a party of Cheyennes on their way to raid the Utes had forcibly entered their homes and looted, stealing such goods as they could carry away.[7]

Lieutenant Hawkins of the Colorado First was dispatched with twenty men in pursuit of the Indians. After a three-day march, Hawkins came upon a village of twenty-one lodges on Bijou Creek, about seventy-five miles from the place of robbery. The Indians were under the leadership of Red Horse, a minor chief, who claimed his innocence and referred Hawkins to another band. Forage was scarce, however, and the troops were forced to return to camp. Hawkins reported, "The Indians talk very bitterly of the whites—say they have stolen their ponies and abused their women, taken their hunting

[5] Susan Riley Ashley, "Reminiscences of Colorado in the Early 'Sixties," *The Colorado Magazine*, Vol. XIII (1936), 222–23.

[6] *Annual Report* of the Commissioner of Indian Affairs, 1863, pp. 252–53. George Bent said that Black Kettle's first wife was captured by the Utes in 1849. Letter from George Bent to Colonel Tappan, February 23, 1889. (Copy in Colorado State Historical Society Library.)

[7] *Annual Report* of the Commissioner of Indian Affairs, 1863, p. 240.

grounds, and that they expected that they would have to fight for their rights."[8]

Another violation by the Indians occurred when a band of Arapahoes stole several head of cattle from a rancher named Van Wormer, thirty-five miles east of Denver. They also took some horses and robbed some white men of their provisions. Van Wormer investigated, visiting a village of Arapahoes on the South Platte, fourteen miles below Denver. A squaw man named North was with them and interpreted for Van Wormer. The Indians frankly admitted to butchering some of the rancher's cattle and even produced a horse which they had stolen. The horse did not belong to Van Wormer, but he took it to Denver and advertised for its owner.[9]

Along the Arkansas, conflicts between the Indians and the whites had been increasing. With the Comanches and Kiowas striking with vengeance along the Santa Fe road, it was often difficult to accurately fix the blame for depredations. The first Cheyenne misconduct along the river reportedly took place on December 5, 1862, when a party of young men attacked the stage station of Cotterel, Viceroy & Company, United States mail contractors, burned a lot of hay, and took provisions, but killed no one. Governor Evans ordered Agent Colley at Fort Lyon to arrest the violators through their chiefs, but by then the guilty ones were long gone.[10]

[8] *Ibid.*

[9] *Ibid.*, pp. 543–44.

[10] *Ibid.*, pp. 239–40.

William H. Ryus, a stagecoach driver of this line, many years later wrote of an incident which supposedly occurred between Larned and Lyon when an unnamed band of hungry Indians approached a wagon train and demanded food and coffee. The wagonmaster refused them, and a frightened teamster shot and wounded one of the Indians. That night the Indians returned and massacred the entire train, with the exception of one man who escaped to

William Bent, in 1865, testified concerning another conflict which took place sometime in the 1862–63 period:

> About three years ago the Arapahoes were encamped near
> Fort Lyon; a soldier had obtained some whiskey and went to
> the Arapaho village after dark; he met an Indian or two out-
> side and told them he wanted a squaw for the whiskey; that is,
> he wanted a squaw to sleep with for the whiskey. The Indian
> told him that if he would give him the whiskey he would get
> him a squaw; he gave him the whiskey, and the Indian started
> off and went into a lodge of his friends, and commenced drink-
> ing the whiskey with them, without bringing the squaw. The
> soldier started on a search for the Indian and whiskey, and
> found them in a lodge. The Indian refused to return the whis-
> key, when the soldier pulled out his revolver, fired and broke
> the Indian's arm; the soldier then made his escape and could
> never be identified by his officers or by the Indians. The matter
> created great confusion among the Indians, but was finally
> settled without a fight.[11]

Whatever isolated conflicts might have occurred, the Southern Cheyenne and Arapaho tribes were still at peace with the
whites in 1863. Samuel G. Colley,[12] who had arrived at Lyon

---

Fort Larned. This affair, which took place seventy-five miles west of Larned,
was known as the Nine Mile Ridge Massacre, according to Ryus. Though there
is a lack of supporting record and though Ryus is often not entirely correct—
he refers to Major Colley as "Macauley"—there is likely some foundation to his
account. William H. Ryus, *The Second William Penn*, 16–20.

11 "The Chivington Massacre," in *Report of the Joint Special Committee
Appointed under Resolution of March 3, 1865*, 93. (In subsequent references
this document will be cited as "The Chivington Massacre.")

12 Samuel G. Colley was appointed agent for the Cheyenne and Arapaho
Indians by Lincoln. He came from Wisconsin where he played an important
role in the settlement of Beloit, serving in the state legislature and as sheriff of
his county. His performance as agent suffered much criticism. Bent and others
claimed that Colley and his son, Dexter, with the help of John Smith, were

in 1861 to replace Boone as Indian agent, dispatched John Smith out to urge the Indians to get together and send a delegation to see the Great Father in Washington. The Indians, who were in an extremely destitute condition, hungry and disease-ridden, were pleased with the idea.

On March 27, 1863, a delegation made up of chiefs from the Cheyenne, Comanche, Arapaho, Kiowa, and Caddoe tribes visited Washington, D. C., where they met President Lincoln. Representing the Cheyennes were War Bonnet, Standing in the Water, and Lean Bear.[13] Though the trip to Washington served to strengthen the bonds of friendship between the Union and the Indian chiefs, the situation was growing worse daily on the plains and by summer was threatening to erupt into a war.

During the absence of the Colorado First to New Mexico, a second regiment of Colorado men, the Second Colorado Volunteers, had been raised by Colonel Jesse H. Leavenworth, West Pointer and son of the man for whom Fort Leavenworth had been named.[14] For a time these troops had been stationed

trading the Indians their own annuities. The Indians substantiated this charge later, though Colley was never formally accused. Ryus in *The Second William Penn* (49–55) tells of a "Macauley" who conspired to condemn the Indians' goods and sell them for a profit. Julia Lambert, wife of the Fort Lyon stationmaster, describes how Mrs. Colley supposedly used annuity flour to bake pies which she sold to Fort Lyon troops. "Plain Tales of the Plains," *The Trail*, Vol. IX (1916), 17–18.

[13] Washington *Daily National Intelligencer*, March 28, 1863. The primary purpose of this visit was to offset the overtures being made by the Confederates in attempts to stir up the Plains tribes into a general war against the settlements in Union-controlled Kansas, Nebraska, and Colorado.

[14] Jesse Henry Leavenworth was born at Danville, Vermont, March 29, 1807. He was appointed to the Military Academy, graduating in 1830, and was assigned to the Fourth Infantry as a second lieutenant. Though he resigned his commission in 1831, he was held in the service by the influence of his father and went on to serve in the Black Hawk War against the Sac Indians in 1832.

at Fort Lyon, but when the First came home, the Second was moved on to Fort Larned, where it was assigned the Herculean task of protecting travel along the Santa Fe Trail. On June 11, 1863, Colonel Leavenworth wrote from a camp thirty miles from Larned that a large body of Comanches were at the Big Bend with from three to four thousand horses, many of them big American animals. He reported, also, that a large number of the Mexican trains bound for New Mexico were loaded with whisky, and he feared the effect of it upon the Indians.[15]

Leavenworth was much annoyed with Chivington for holding so many troops in Denver when they could be helping him patrol the Santa Fe Trail. He complained to departmental headquarters in regard to this, and at the same time made a request to Lt. Colonel Tappan,[16] now commanding Fort Lyon,

In 1836 he again resigned his commission and went to Chicago, where he was employed as a civil engineer until 1858, later becoming a lumber merchant and moving to Wisconsin. In 1860 he went to Colorado, and on February 17, 1862, he was appointed a colonel and was authorized to recruit a second regiment of volunteers in Colorado. He arrived back in Denver on June 2, 1862, at the head of 150 men and a battery of six brass guns which had been captured at Fort Donelson. Carolyn Thomas Foreman, "Col. Jesse Henry Leavenworth," *Chronicles of Oklahoma,* Vol. XIII (1935), 14–29.

15 *War of the Rebellion Official Records of the Union and Confederate Armies,* Series I, Vol. XXII, Part II, 316–17. (In subsequent references this work will be cited as *Rebellion Records.*)

16 Samuel F. Tappan came to Colorado Territory via the Kansas border wars. As one of the original founders of Lawrence in 1854, he had soon become one of the central figures in the heated conflict between the Free Staters and the proslavery factions in Kansas. A man of literary ability, Tappan served as a correspondent for the New York *Tribune* and Boston *Atlas.* In 1855 he and another man made a canvass of southern and western Kansas in favor of the Free State movement, and in 1856 he was clerk of the Topeka Constitutional Convention. Later he was secretary of the ill-fated Leavenworth Constitutional Convention of 1858 and clerk of the Wyndotte Convention of 1859 which adopted the constitution still in use in Kansas today. In July of 1860 he joined

for assistance.[17] Chivington strongly resented this encroachment upon his command, and on June 23 he sent definite instructions to Tappan through Lieutenant Soule, his adjutant, "You will not, therefore, send or go with your forces to Larned, or indeed out of the district, except for temporary purposes. ... Colonel L. has no authority to call for troops from this district, and will not have.[18]

In the meantime, at Fort Larned, Leavenworth was having considerable trouble over the killing of a Cheyenne by a guard there. The Indian was Little Heart, who was drunk and headed for the fort to secure more whisky.[19] He tried to ride over the guard and was shot and killed. Leavenworth's report of July 15 gives a full picture of his situation:

> On the morning of the 9th instant, a sentinel on post at this fort (Larned) shot and killed an Indian. It was about 1 A. M. As we were surrounded by all the Apache, Arapaho, and Kiowa Indians, and not knowing to which tribe he belonged, our position was rather unpleasant, owing to not having many troops here; and, as the Indians had been troublesome on the Santa Fe road, I had out on scout some 50 of our small garrison, to protect trains above and below on the river. As soon as this Indian was killed, I sent runners out for all the scouts to return to the post, and called a council of all the chiefs. By

the gold rush to Colorado. As second in command of the Colorado Volunteers at La Glorieta, he fought well, "Lieut. Col. Tappan sat on his horse during the charge, leisurely loading and firing his pistols as if rabbit hunting." Ovando J. Hollister, *Boldly They Rode, A History of the First Colorado Regiment of Volunteers,* 70.

When Colonel Slough resigned command of the Colorado regiment, Tappan waived his rank in favor of the regiment's popular choice of Chivington as commander. Upon the First's reassignment to Colorado Territory, Tappan was placed in command of Fort Lyon.

[17] *Rebellion Records,* Series I, Vol. XXII, Part II, 172–73, 400–401.
[18] *Ibid.,* 333–34.
[19] George Bird Grinnell, *The Fighting Cheyennes,* 132.

8 A. M. all the chiefs (principal chiefs) were here. As I had told
the runners to inform the chiefs I did not want any braves or
other Indians to visit the post, all kept away but the Kiowas;
they could not be governed by their chiefs, and came up in
strong force, and very much excited; more so than any Indians
I ever saw. Upon examination of the dead Indian by the chiefs,
it was found to be a Cheyenne; they happened to be in small
numbers, and we happily escaped a collision for the moment.
What may happen is impossible for me to say.[20]

Leavenworth managed to smooth the matter over without
incident, though it was to have later consequences in affairs
with the Cheyennes. Even before he finished his report on
the subject, however, the Fort Lyon mail messenger arrived
with word that was the beginning of a long-standing enmity
between Leavenworth and Chivington. Leavenworth wrote,
"The Fort Lyon mail is in, and the messenger informs me that
he applied for an escort to the mail to the commanding officer
of a company of the First Colorado Cavalry, but he refused to
send a man with him. . . . Am I expected to guard and escort
trains on the whole of this road, for 400 miles, with but one
company of cavalry?"[21]

Upon learning of the Indian disturbance, however, Tappan
did send reinforcements to Larned. When Chivington learned
of it, he removed Tappan from command at Lyon. On July
22, Leavenworth wrote to Major General E. V. Sumner, now
commanding the Department of the Missouri, ". . . I ask as a
great favor of the general commanding this district that he

[20] *Rebellion Records,* Series I, Vol. XXII, Part II, 400–401.

The *Rocky Mountain News* of October 14, 1863, reported: ". . . Col. Leavenworth, with the utmost coolness and bravery, left the entrenchments and
went among them [the Indians], alone and unarmed, called the chiefs around
him and succeeded in pacifying them. . . ."

[21] *Rebellion Records,* Series I, Vol. XXII, Part II, 401–402.

will so represent our matters out here to General Schofield as will not only restore Colonel Tappan to his former command, but place his post, and the whole of the Santa Fe road, without the District of Colorado, if Col. J. M. Chivington is to command it any longer."[22]

As a result of Leavenworth's complaint, Chivington was called upon by Schofield to defend his need for troops against representations that a regiment could then be spared from the District of Colorado. Chivington replied "Colorado, in my judgment, is not of second importance to any State or Territory to the General Government. If protected and kept quiet she will yield twenty millions of gold this year, and double yearly in years to come, and in view of the national debt, I think this important, very!"[23]

Chivington won his point, and neither was Fort Lyon removed from his command then nor was Tappan returned to that post, being sent instead to out-of-the-way Fort Garland.[24]

[22] *Ibid.*

[23] *Ibid.*, 527–29.

[24] Following this incident, District Inspector Major Downing filed numerous reports to the Department of Kansas accusing Tappan of gross neglect, of defying Lincoln by employing a prisoner as a clerk, of spitting in Lincoln's eye by retaining Lieutenant Baldwin after that officer had brought in the dismembered head of the Mexican desperado Espinosas, of allowing the Fort Garland post to become drunk and uproarious. But General Curtis stood firm, noting, "The desire to get Lt. Col. Tappan mustered out by summary proceedings has already been rebuked. The Major [Downing] as Inspector is after his Lt. Col. and efforts have been made to use this sort of [undecipherable] til it seemed preposterous."

Tappan retorted to the attacks with a bitter letter to the Department, "I am reliably informed that upon the return of Capain S. M. Robbins, Chief of Cavalry for Colorado to Denver from a tour of Inspection of this post he made a report upon my qualifications as an officer which was not satisfactory to Colonel J. M. Chivington Commanding the District, and Major Downing, District Inspector, both of whom proposed to Captain Robbins that if he would

Leavenworth meanwhile was having other troubles. Having been given the authority when recruiting the second regiment to appoint the officers of the regiment, he had incurred much hard feeling. In August when the command was ordered to Fort Lyon, another difficulty arose. Leavenworth had authorized W. D. McLane to recruit an artillery company, promising them service as artillery support of the Second. However, when the time for mustering in came, the order embraced only infantry and the men refused to accept this status. They appealed through channels to Washington, and, as a result, in October Leavenworth and three of his officers were suddenly dishonorably discharged from the service. A subsequent review of the facts by Judge Advocate Holt, however, caused the discharge to be changed to an honorable one. On October 19, 1863, Leavenworth turned over the command of Fort Larned to Captain J. W. Parmetar of the Twelfth Kansas Volunteers, and the command of the Second was assigned to Lieutenant Colonel Dodd.[25]

report me unqualified for my position and advise my dismissal from the service they would secure his promotion as a reward for his perfidy to a majority vacated by the promotion of Downing to the Lt-colonelcy made vacant by my dismissal and if he did not make such a report they would do all they could to prevent his further advancement in the regiment. Captain Robbins declined this infamous proposal." From a dispatch from Lieutenant Colonel Samuel Tappan to Colonel J. V. Dubois, Chief of Cavalry, Department of the Missouri, January 10, 1864. Tappan A.G.O. File.

Tappan later recalled a letter to General Curtis, which evidently denounced Downing and Chivington, as he felt that airing the charges during wartime would not be to the best interests of the regiment. Curtis sent it back.

[25] A Third Colorado Regiment had been raised, and Colonel James H. Ford was put in command. This unit was moved to Missouri, and in December of 1863 it was integrated as a part of the Second Regiment with Ford commanding. This Third Regiment thus ceased to exist and is not to be confused with the Third Regiment of hundred-day volunteers formed in the fall of 1864. *The Denver Republican,* May 11, 1890, p. 14.

In May of 1863, Governor Evans had received word that the Cheyenne and Arapaho tribes were holding a big secret conference with the Sioux about one hundred miles north of Denver for the purpose of uniting and driving the white man from the country.[26] In response to this report, Evans sent for the chiefs of a large Arapaho village then camped seventy-five miles north of Denver, and told them that "if they went to war with the whites it would be a war of extermination to them."[27] He asked them to pass the word around.

Evans sent Elbridge Gerry,[28] a Sioux squaw man who had a ranch north of Denver, in search of the Indian tribes to arrange for a peace council. At the same time, Agent Colley and John Smith were trying to get the Arkansas River Indians to attend the council, but the Indians said their horses were too poor, the trip too long, and they were busy making their lodges. Gerry left Denver on July 29 with a wagon and four-mule team carrying goods and provisions for treating with the Indians.[29]

The Cheyennes were on their summer buffalo hunt, and Gerry found 150 lodges, all Cheyenne, on the head of the Smoky Hill Fork of the Kansas River. He distributed the goods, then called a council of the chiefs, telling them of Governor Evans' wish to hold a peace meeting. The chiefs were reluctant. Their hunt had been going well, and they had no desire to talk with the white chief, but finally they agreed to meet Evans on September 29.

26 *Rebellion Records,* Series I, Vol. XXII, Part II, 294.

27 *Annual Report* of the Commissioner of Indian Affairs, 1863, pp. 239–46.

28 Evans described Gerry: ". . . . he is a grandson of Elbridge Gerry who signed the Declaration of Independence, and a scholar and a man of very good mind." "The Chivington Massacre," 46.

29 *Annual Report* of the Commissioner of Indian Affairs, 1863, pp. 247–48.

Gerry then returned to Denver and escorted Evans, Colley, and Sioux Agent Lorey to the junction of the Arickaree and Cherry forks of the Republican where they met four lodges of Indians, who reported that the main body of the Cheyennes were on their way to council. Gerry left the commissioners on September 6 and proceeded to the council grounds, but found no Indians. A search up Beaver Creek for about twenty-five miles turned up nothing, so the next day Gerry rode back to the place where he had previously met with the Cheyennes. They were still in camp there, their lodges now increased to 240, constituting a sizeable portion of the Southern Cheyenne tribe. The Dog Soldiers[30] were with them.

Gerry called a council to ask why the Indians had not kept their promise to meet the white chief. They explained their reason—their camps were ravaged by whooping cough and diarrhea, and even during the time that Gerry had been gone, thirty-five of their children had died.

They went on to state further that they were unhappy about the treaty of Fort Wise, which they considered a swindle. It was claimed that Black Kettle—who was in camp, but too ill to attend the council—and White Antelope both denied having signed it, and insisted that those who did sign had not understood it. The buffalo, they said, would last a hundred years yet, and the Cheyennes would not leave their hunting grounds to go to a reservation where there was no game. They also denied that they had sold the country at the headwaters of the Republican and Smoky Hill and would not give it up.

[30] The Dog Soldiers were originally a group of Cheyennes outcast from the main tribe, but during this period they were largely the main warrior contingent and were powerful through their influence on the young men of the various Cheyenne bands.

32

The whites had taken the North Platte country, and the Cheyennes claimed only the country at the head of the Republican and Smoky Hill. As for railroads, the whites could build them across their country as long as they did not settle along them. This they would not allow.

They pointed to the recent killing of the Cheyenne brave at Fort Larned as proof that the white man's hand dripped with blood. This was still a touchy matter with the Cheyennes, for the guard had been an Osage Indian in the service of the government, and the tribe felt insulted that the government would take sides against them in favor of another tribe.

Evans was forced to return to Denver, disgruntled that the Indians had not met with him. Upon returning to the city, he received a report from the squaw man North[31] concerning Indian hostility:

Having recovered an Arapaho prisoner, a squaw, from the Utes, I obtained the confidence of the Indians completely. I have lived with them from a boy, and my wife is an Arapaho. In honor of my exploit in recovering the prisoner the Indians recently gave me a 'big medicine dance' about 55 miles below Fort Lyon, on the Arkansas River, at which the leading chiefs and warriors of several of the tribes of the plains met. The Comanches, Apaches, Kiowas, the northern band of Arapahoes, and all of the Cheyennes, with the Sioux, have pledged one another to go to war with the whites as soon as they can procure ammunition in the spring. I heard them discuss the matter often and the few of them who opposed it were forced to be quiet and were really in danger of the loss of their lives.

I saw the principal chiefs pledge to each other that they

[31] Robert North led a group of Arapaho hostiles in the massacre of eighty soldiers near Fort Phil Kearny in 1866. He was supposedly hanged by renegades in 1869, along with his Arapaho wife, while on his way to a Southern Arapaho camp.

would shake hands and be friendly with the whites until they procured ammunition and guns, so as to be ready when they strike. Plundering to get means has already commenced, and the plan is to commence war at several points in the sparse settlements early in the spring.[32]

Nine days later Evans met with Roman Nose and two or three minor chiefs of the Arapaho tribes who professed friendship on their own part but declared that there "is a hostility and a disposition to war on the part of the Cheyennes, Sioux, and Kiowas."[33] Roman Nose refused to enter into any treaty with Evans.

Replacing Tappan in command of Fort Lyon was Major Scott J. Anthony, who in September reported that the Kiowas and Comanches had been committing depredations near the Cimarron Crossing. Three trains had arrived at the fort destitute of provisions, and a trainmaster said they were robbed by Indians, some of which held white prisoners.

Toward the last of September, Anthony led a command down the river as far as Larned, taking along John Smith as interpreter. He visited the camps of the Kiowas, Comanches, Apaches, Caddoes, and Arapahoes, who all professed friendship but said that the Sioux were trying to get them united for an attack on the Platte and Arkansas roads.

The Arapahoes under Little Raven, Left Hand, and Neva were moving toward Lyon with two thousand Indians, very diseased, destitute, and hungry. There were also some five hundred Caddoes from Texas moving in the direction of the post, but they reportedly had adopted the customs of the whites and were well behaved.[34]

[32] *Rebellion Records,* Series I, Vol. XXXIV, Part IV, 100.
[33] *Annual Report* of the Commissioner of Indian Affairs, 1863, pp. 540–41.

By late 1863 preparations were under way to begin construction work on the agency under the provisions of the treaty of Fort Wise. Because of irrigation advantages, the agency was moved upriver to the Point of Rocks,[35] a few miles above Bent's Old Fort. Here a blacksmith's house and shop were constructed and a warehouse begun, with plans under way for building an agent's house, which would include a council room. An irrigation ditch was commenced and completed the following spring, at which time some 250 acres of corn were planted.

During the winter of 1863, however, this effort did the Indians little good. Colley reported there were no buffalo within two hundred miles of the reservation and but little game of any kind. "Most of the depredations committed by them are from starvation. It is hard to make them understand that they have no right to take from them that have, when in a starving condition."[36]

Major Anthony was less compassionate about the welfare of the tribes. He wrote, "The Indians are all very destitute this season, and the government will be compelled to subsist them to a great extent, or allow them to starve to death, which would probably be much the easier way of disposing of them."[37]

[34] *Rebellion Records,* Series I, Vol. XXII, Part II, 507.

[35] *Annual Report* of the Commissioner of Indian Affairs, 1864, p. 393. There were several landmarks in the area known as "Point of Rocks." One of these was directly across the Arkansas from Fort Lyon (old), and has often been mistakenly identified as the site of the agency.

[36] *Annual Report* of the Commissioner of Indian Affairs, 1863.

[37] *Rebellion Records,* Series I, Vol. XXII, Part II, 571.

III.

WAR
WITH THE
CHEYENNES

In the spring of 1864 war with the Cheyennes came, but not as North had led Evans to believe it would come—as a co-ordinated attack by a confederation of the Plains tribes. There was, in fact, neither confederation nor attack. The Indian war of 1864 was commenced when two cases of cattle theft by Indians were reported and troops were ordered out, not merely to investigate the reports but to capture and punish violators. These punitive expeditions led to conflicts with the Indians, conflicts which were compounded by a philosophy of a "war of extermination" on the part of the white troops.

On April 12, 1864, an engagement occurred between a company of fifteen mounted troops under the command of Lieutenant Dunn, First Colorado Cavalry, and a small band of Cheyennes.[1] This affair, which took place three miles from

Fremont's Orchard on the South Platte, was later defined by Black Kettle and White Antelope as the beginning of the war.

On April 11 a rancher named Ripley came into Camp Sanborn, on the Platte trail, with the report that Indians were stealing stock along Bijou Creek, tearing down telegraph lines, and driving people from ranches along the creek. Early the next day, Lieutenant Dunn and forty men of Companies C and H, First Colorado, galloped out of Camp Sanborn with orders to pursue the Indians, disarm them, and recover the stock. They took Ripley along as a guide.

After leaving the camp Dunn divided his command, sending half of the troops directly to Ripley's ranch on Bijou Creek, taking the remainder himself to scout along the sandy hills and ravine-slashed country along the Platte to its junction with the Bijou. Finding no sign of Indians, Dunn turned toward the Bijou ranch, making contact with the other half of the command around two in the afternoon. Shortly afterward the command picked up an Indian trail and began following it until within three miles of the South Platte, where they sighted a column of smoke to the right of the trail ahead.

Once again Dunn divided his forces, sending half of them into the sand hills in the direction of the smoke and continuing on the trail with the balance of the troops. His horses having traveled some distance without water, Dunn halted at the Platte, some three miles above Fremont's Orchard, and

[1] This account is based on the following sources: *Rebellion Records,* Series I, Vol. XXXIV, Part I, 883 (report of Captain George L. Sanborn, Camp Sanborn, April 12, 1864); *ibid.,* 884–85, 887–88 (reports of Lieutenant Clark Dunn, Camp Sanborn, April 18, 1864); "The Chivington Massacre, 72–73 (affidavit of Mr. Bouser); *Senate Executive Documents,* 39th Cong., 2d sess., No. 26 ("Sand Creek Massacre"), 180–82, (testimony of Lieutenant Clark Dunn). (In subsequent references this document will be cited as "Sand Creek Massacre.")

allowed the animals to water. During this stop at around four in the afternoon, Dunn's force spotted a party of fifteen to twenty Indians crossing the river about a mile upstream. Another smaller party of Indians was seen driving a herd of horses toward the bluffs north of the Platte.

Dunn continued to water his horses, sending Ripley and a soldier across the river to have a look at the stock. Presently they returned, and Ripley claimed that they were his animals which the Indians had. He also informed Dunn that the main body of Indians were drawing into a line up the river, evidently preparing for a fight. Crossing the river, the Lieutenant found this to be true. The Indians were lined up waiting for him.[2]

Dispatching Ripley and four of his troops to go after the stock, leaving him with fifteen men besides himself, Dunn formed his command into a line and approached to within five hundred yards of the Indians. At this point Dunn dismounted and walked to the front of his troops, motioning for the Indians to send a man out to parley. Dunn's men, fearing for his safety, called for him to come back.

[2] Dunn claimed that the Indians were evidently intending to steal a horse and mule herd grazing near Fremont's Orchard, which belonged to the quartermaster at Denver. *Rebellion Records,* Series I, Vol. XXXIV, Part I, 884–85.

A Sioux squaw man named Bouser, who interpreted for Governor Evans, gave this account of what the Indians were doing with the stock: "I know an Indian named Spotted Horse, part Cheyenne and part Sioux; he is now dead; he told me that he was in the affair with Lieutenant Dunn. He said that the Indians took three head of cattle, there were 100 warriors. There was snow on the ground, and the Indians were hungry and took the cattle; they would have come into Denver if their horses had been in condition. They went south of the river with the cattle, intending if the soldiers came after them to settle for the cattle by giving some of their ponies. Before they had time to cross the river and kill the cattle the soldiers overtook them." "The Chivington Massacre," 72–73.

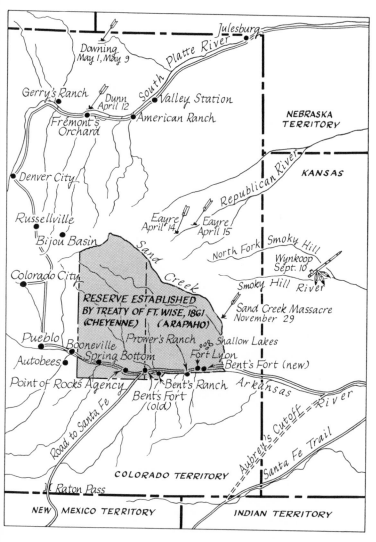

BEGINNING OF THE CHEYENNE WAR OF 1864

After some talk among the Indians, one of the braves rode forward to shake hands with Dunn. Eventually all of them came forward and began shaking hands with the soldiers, some of whom had dismounted. At this point Dunn demanded that the Indians turn over the stock and thought to disarm them according to his instructions. But to separate a Plains Indian from his weapon was not as simple as it may have seemed to Dunn. When he reached out to take the gun of one of the bucks, the move was an automatic violation of friendship and a signal for a fight.

Immediately the Indians commenced running and firing back at the soldiers, who quickly began returning the fire. A running engagement followed, the soldiers pursuing the Indians about fifteen miles. Captain Sanborn, to whom Dunn reported immediately afterward, wrote that "Lieutenant Dunn has just arrived and reports that none of the men were killed; several of the Indians were seen to fall from their horses, but being freshly mounted, succeeded in getting them away. . . ."[3]

The battle lasted from one-half to three-quarters of an hour, the Indians retreating into the bluffs and easily outdistancing the spent cavalry horses. Four of Dunn's men were wounded: J. G. Brandly had an arrowhead in his back; R. E. McBride had two severe wounds from arrows in his back, one opposite the right lung; A. J. Baird was wounded by an arrow in the right shoulder; and John Crosby's right arm was broken between the shoulder and elbow by a pistol ball. Brandly and Baird later died.

While Dunn claimed that he killed some eight or ten of the Indians and wounded about twelve or fifteen more, the

[3] *Rebellion Records,* Series I, Vol. XXXIV, Part I, 883.

Indians said that only three braves were wounded.[4] At first
Dunn did not know what tribe of Indians he had encountered,
and bows were sent to Denver for identification. In his report,
Dunn stated that the Indians were armed with rifles, Navy
and Dragoon pistols, and carbine pistols, in addition to their
bows and arrows.[5] The Indians' side of the story was given by
Lieutenant Cramer after hearing it from Black Kettle that
year on the Smoky Hill:

At first a good deal of stock was stolen from the Indians by
the whites, over on or out near the Platte country. Previous to
the fight with the soldiers in the vicinity of the Platte (by
description supposed to be the command of Lieutenant
Dunn) that they were travelling from the Smoky Hill country
and found some loose stock, I think, on the Beaver or Box
Elder, and took it with them to leave at Geary's ranch, and on
arriving there found no one at home and took the stock with
them. Soon after this they were overtaken by a party of
soldiers who appeared to be friendly, but demanded the stock
which they had in their possession which they were willing to
give up, and offered to do so with the exception of one horse
or mule, which they stated to the chief of the soldiers one of
the Indians had off on a hunt and would be back in a day or
two, and as soon as he returned, the mule or horse should be
given up. The chief of the soldiers still demanded the mule or
horse, at the same time taking from the Indians their arms,
which the Indians supposed were merely to look at. One of
the Indians refused to let him take his arms, when he undertook to take them by force. I am not positive that the Indians
fired first, but my impression is that he [Black Kettle] said the
Indians fired first after the attempt to take arms by force. I

4 Grinnell, *The Fighting Cheyennes,* 142.

5 It almost appears that the soldiers would have been better off had the
Indians possessed more guns and fewer bows and arrows.

think that the Indians stated there were three killed or wounded.[6]

Dunn and his force arrived back at Camp Sanborn, twenty miles from the battle site, at midnight. Obtaining fresh horses and with Gerry for a guide, they set out again at daylight on the morning of April 14, following the trail until noon when the weather turned—storming, snowing, and blowing until the trail became obliterated. On the advice of Gerry, Dunn turned back, reaching camp before daylight the next morning.

That night a report arrived at the camp that the Indians which Dunn had fought had come back and taken a herd of cattle from a ranch on Beaver Creek, killed two herders, and wounded the owner, a man named Bradley, in the neck with an arrow.[7] Within half an hour, Dunn, Lieutenant Chase, and thirty men were in the saddle once more with four days' rations. They went to Bijou Ranch, thence to Dry Creek, and finally to Junction Ranch where they picked up Samuel Ashcraft, an old squaw man, as a guide. Finding a trail, they followed it until around noon, when they reached the ranch

[6] "Sand Creek Massacre," 32.

Bouser's account is as follows: "The soldiers had no interpreter, held no talk with the Indians, gave them no time even to deliver the cattle, but pitched into them. He also told me that had he been up in time, as he speaks English, or had there been an interpreter, the whole matter might have been settled without a fight. As it was, the Indians rode up close to the soldiers, dismounted, and shook hands with them. Lieutenant Dunn's men then took hold of some of the Indians' weapons and tried to wrest them away. The Indians did not know what it meant, and refused to give up their arms, when they were fired upon by the soldiers. Spotted Horse, seeing that there was going to be a war, threw up his chieftainship, and with it some one hundred head of ponies, and came into Governor Evans. I acted as interpreter, and he told substantially to Governor Evans the above." "The Chivington Massacre," 72–73.

[7] *Rebellion Records*, Series I, Vol. XXXIV, Part III, 167.

on Beaver Creek where the white men were supposed to have been murdered. They not only found no dead men, but not even signs of a struggle.

Still following the Indians' trail the command came across about forty head of cattle which they supposed the Indians had bypassed. The troops secured the cattle, then followed the trail southeastward, riding all night up the left fork of Beaver Creek to its headwaters. Finally Ashcraft suggested that the Indians must have headed for the Arkansas River, and Dunn, deciding his horses were too worn to follow, returned regretfully to Camp Sanborn, arriving on April 16.

During the march Dunn and his men had been in the saddle for sixty hours, traveling some 250 miles.

Chivington received Sanborn's report on Dunn's fight with the Indians and immediately wired orders to Lieutenant Hawkins at Camp Collins to send a strong detachment out to intercept the Indians, instructing him to, "Be sure you have the right ones, and then kill them."[8]

On April 16, Major Jacob Downing was ordered to Camp Sanborn to take charge of movements against the Indians and see that "they are appropriately chastised for their outlawry."[9] Two days later a messenger arrived at the camp with the report that a party of Cheyennes had taken possession of a ranch along the Platte and were getting drunk and driving off the white people.[10]

[8] *Ibid.,* 151.

[9] *Ibid.,* 189. Captain Logan of the First Colorado had arrived at Fort Cottonwood on the Platte on April 9 after making a tour of the South Platte to check on the condition of things. On April 16 a parley was held with the Sioux at Fort Cottonwood by General Mitchell in an inconclusive effort at a treaty.

[10] *Ibid.,* 242–43.

43

Within an hour Downing had sixty men in the saddle, heading east along the South Platte, and found that inhabitants along the river were very frightened that an Indian war had broken out.[11] They reported having seen ten Cheyenne lodges. Shortly after noon the following day Downing arrived at Indian Ranch, some fifty-five miles east of Camp Sanborn, but found no evidence of Cheyennes, though his scouts reported several Sioux lodges seven miles below the ranch. Since the Sioux were reported to be friendly at that time, Downing did not bother them.

On the return march, guide Gerry reported that he had spotted an Indian watching their movements. Downing sent Gerry out with a patrol to investigate; but, though they found a fresh trail of three or four Indians, they came up with nothing. The command returned to camp on April 20. Following this fruitless venture, Downing decided upon a campaign to punish the Indians along the river. "My object," Downing reported to Chivington, "is to protect the immigration and get as many together as possible, when, if you think proper, a command can go to their village and compel them to surrender the depredators, or clean them out."[12]

He decided, also, that he could have a better center of operations by moving down-river to Junction Ranch. There, on April 26, he received a report of a force of Cheyennes below, who had stolen about $800 worth of horses from a ranch down the Platte. The soldiers pursued the Indians twenty-five miles south toward the Republican River where they found eleven lodges, only recently abandoned. These lodges, along with cooking utensils, implements for dressing

11 *Ibid.*
12 *Ibid.*, 250–52.

44

hides, and other paraphernalia were destroyed, and a large number of buffalo hides captured. Scouts reported that the Indians' trail led south toward the Republican.

On May 2 Downing reported to Chivington again, this time from the American Ranch:

> Yesterday we took an Indian prisoner, whom I at first ordered shot, but upon learning from one of my men that he was half Sioux and had received his annuities from the Government with the Sioux, I concluded to spare him if he would lead me to a Cheyenne camp or give me information of their whereabouts, which he has consented to do, and we are about starting in pursuit. Besides, all concured that if I killed him it would involve the Sioux, which, as I understand, the policy is to avoid a war with them. If, though, I obeyed my own impulse, I would kill him. Should he attempt to escape will settle him.[13]

With the Sioux leading the way, Downing and Dunn marched from American Ranch at 2:00 P.M. the same day with about forty men, traveling some fifteen miles and resting, then hitting the trail again and marching all night.[14] Early in the morning, shortly after sunrise, the troops found a Cheyenne camp in a canyon near Cedar Bluffs, sixty miles from American Ranch.

Downing immediately threw his force between the Indian camp and their horse herd. Detailing ten men to take charge of the herd, he dismounted three companies and with twenty-five men began fighting on foot. After a few exchanges of fire the Indians retreated into a canyon, which provided them a natural fortification, and held it. After about an hour, during

[13] *Ibid.*, 407.
[14] *Rebellion Records*, Series I, Vol. XXXIV, Part I, 907–908.

which time, so Downing claimed, the soldiers killed about twenty-five Indians and wounded thirty or forty more, the carbine ammunition began running low, and Downing withdrew to American Ranch with about a hundred captured Indian ponies, which he distributed among the boys.[15]

The soldiers had one man killed and one wounded. Downing reported, "Though I think we have punished them pretty severely in this affair, yet I believe now it is but the commencement of war with this tribe, which must result in exterminating them."[16]

Within a week's time Downing had reoutfitted and headed back to Cedar Canyon for another fight, this time with eighty men. On this occasion, however, the Indians were not surprised and decamped, leaving behind their lodges, fourteen in number, which Downing burned.[17]

Shortly afterward Downing came across a large encampment of Sioux, who said that the Cheyennes had asked them for help to fight the soldiers and the Sioux had refused. They also said that a Cheyenne war party had headed for the Platte to steal horses. Downing went there but found no Indians.

The Indians' side of this affair was also told by Lieutenant Cramer:

The Indians then went to Cedar Bluffs immediately after this occurence [their fight with Dunn at Fremont's Orchard]. Soon after they were attacked by another party of soldiers. Before the attack and while in camp at or near Cedar Bluffs, one of their herders, a boy, was killed, and another captured . . . and a number of their herd of stock; I think he said near a

15 "The Chivington Massacre," 69.
16 *Rebellion Records*, Series I, Vol. XXXIV, Part I, 907–908.
17 *Ibid.*, 916.

hundred. . . . The Indians then became convinced the whites were going to make war on them and prepared to go to the Arkansas valley; had left a good deal of their property; had rolled up what they could and hid them in the rocks, and while preparing to start were attacked by a party of soldiers, killing one. I do not recollect that he [Black Kettle] said any were wounded or not; that he thought the soldiers were firing on buffalo-robes in the rocks, and not at the Indians; that they immediately after started for the Arkansas valley. . . .[18]

John Smith's testimony parallels Cramer's:

A short time after this occurence [Dunn's fight] took place, a village of squaws, papooses and old men, located at what is known as "Cedar Cañon," a short distance north of the South Platte, who were perfectly unaware of any difficulty having occurred between any portion of their tribe (Cheyenne) and the whites, were attacked by a large party of soldiers and some of them killed and their ponies driven off.[19]

While Dunn and Downing were chastising the bands along the South Platte, another campaign was being waged against the Cheyennes west of Denver by Lieutenant George S. Eayre, commanding the Independent Battery of Colorado Volunteer Artillery. On April 7, 1864, Eayre, with a detachment of men, was ordered by Chivington in pursuit of Indians who had reportedly stolen 175 head of cattle from Irwin and Jackman, government contractors.[20] Taking the field on the eighth of April with fifty-four men, two twelve-pound moun-

---

[18] "Sand Creek Massacre," 32.

[19] *Ibid.*, 126.

[20] *Rebellion Records*, Series I, Vol. XXXIV, Part I, 880–82.

Grinnell states that the Indians claimed the stock wandered toward their camp and were driven in by some young men out buffalo hunting. Grinnell, *The Fighting Cheyennes*, 138.

tain howitzers, and ten Espenshied wagons under Lieutenant Phillips, he headed southeast out of Denver, camping that night thirty miles southeast of the city.

The eleventh found the command on Beaver Creek, eighty miles southeast of Denver, where a man named Routh, who had been herding cattle in the vicinity of Bijou Basin, joined the command as a guide. During the next day's march Eayre crossed the dividing ridge between the valleys of the South Platte and the Arkansas and encamped on Sand Creek. Here the snow storm which had stopped Dunn forced the command to remain in camp on the thirteenth, but the next day Eayre moved on down Sand Creek some twenty miles and made camp. It was here that he hit an Indian trail with, so Eayre supposed, some hundred head of cattle.

He followed this trail until the headwaters of the Republican were reached, and there a scout reported an Indian village about a mile in advance. Eayre halted his command and dispatched Lieutenant Phillips with two men to make inquiry of the Indians concerning the stolen cattle. One of the men came riding back in about ten minutes and reported that the Indian women were mounted and leaving the village and a force of warriors was headed for the command.

Eayre put his column in motion, and when passing through a defile an Indian was seen standing about fifty yards from them. Eayre ordered two men to take the man prisoner, but as they advanced on him the Indian shot one of the soldiers from his saddle. Eayre reported:

> At this point I ordered the Artillery back to the transports, the nature of the ground being such as to prohibit its farther advance, and divided my forces into squads of 10 men each,

with instructions to scour the country for a distance of 10 miles. Taking 3 men with me I proceeded to the village and found it entirely deserted, but containing immense supplies of beef and buffalo, dried and packed in the manner peculiar to the Indians; also a quantity of undressed buffalo robes, cooking utensils, powder, lead, beads, and all the paraphernalia of a completely supplied Indian village, all of which I burned, except such articles essential for the use of the command, and encamped on the ground.[21]

On the next day, the fifteenth, Eayre continued his course northwestward. His transportation animals (wagon stock) were showing signs of exhaustion, one mule dropping dead in its harness. In order to cross some of the ravines, the soldiers were forced to attach a rope to the wagon tongues and draw the ten-thousand-pound-iron axle wagons over by hand. Fifteen miles from the first village, Eayre came on a second which had also been only recently deserted. Going into camp there, Eayre sent pursuit squads out again but came up with no Indians, though the trail was littered with robes, dried meats, lodges, lodge poles, and other Indian goods. The scouting parties returned with nineteen head of cattle which the guide claimed as part of those which had been stolen. Eayre also put the torch to this village.

Lack of forage for his stock decided Eayre to return to Denver, and on April 22 he submitted these conclusions: "That the Cheyenne Indians are the ones who stole the cattle; that they meditate hostilities against the whites, from the fact of their having first fired upon the command; that they are now encamped upon the Republican, some 200 miles east of Denver. . . ."[22]

21 *Ibid.*
22 *Ibid.*

Dissatisfied with the wagons he was using, Eayre comman-deered fifteen light wagons off the streets of Denver and took to the field after the Indians on the Republican on the twenty-fourth of April. On May 1 he reported to Chivington from a camp on the Smoky Hill, 160 miles southeast of Denver.[23] He stated that he was hot on the trail of a large band of one hundred lodges and was convinced that the Cheyennes were not as yet together as a tribe but roaming the prairie in sep-arate bands. This was the last report to reach Denver from Eayre for some time.

On May 23, Chivington received a telegram from Major O'Brien at Fort Cottonwood, on the Platte Trail in Nebraska, asking, "Is there any of your command out after the Chey-ennes? Reports here are that a whole company are engaged fighting 180 miles south of this post; nearly all killed."[24]

Major Wynkoop at Lyon was instructed to send out a scout-ing party, and O'Brien was requested to do the same. On May 26, Wynkoop's scouting parties had nothing to report. By May 29, Chivington had still not heard from Eayre but felt that, since mails were disrupted by high waters, he need not be too concerned. He wrote to Wynkoop from Denver on that date "Again, I cannot see how it would be possible for his entire command to be cut off; and yet, again, I think it impossible for the Indians to be in such force as to whip him with the arms and men he had, unless he first allowed his command to lie down and go to sleep without any sentinels out, which I think impossible under the instructions I gave him; but, after all, I am somewhat fearful for his safety"[25]

[23] *Rebellion Records,* Series I, Vol. XXXIV, Part IV, 101. Eayre was prob-ably just over the Kansas border now. He had been ordered by Chivington to report in by courier until near Larned or Lyon.

[24] *Ibid.,* 14.

COLONEL JOHN M. CHIVINGTON
First Colorado Cavalry

Courtesy Library, State Historical Society of Colorado

MAJOR SCOTT J. ANTHONY
First Colorado Cavalry

Courtesy Denver Public Library Western Collection

Two days later, however, Chivington received a communication from Eayre at Fort Larned dated May 19 "Sir: I have the honor to inform you that on the 16th instant, when within 3 miles of the Smoky Hill, I was attacked by the Cheyenne Indians, about 400 strong, and after a persistent fight of seven and one-half hours succeeded in driving them from the field. They lost 3 chiefs and 25 warriors killed; the wounded I am unable to estimate. My own loss is 4 men killed and 3 wounded. My animals are exhausted. I will remain at this post until further orders."[26]

Chivington's Adjutant, J. S. Maynard, wrote Eayre that "the colonel commanding district is highly gratified at the conduct of yourself and command, and will so speak of you in his report to department headquarters."[27]

Eayre claims the Indians attacked first, and while this may be so there is much doubt as to who actually started the trouble. Clearly Eayre was out to kill Indians. Wynkoop stated in an affidavit: "Sergeant Fribbley was approached by Lean Bear, and accompanied by him into our column, leaving his warriors at some distance. A short time after Lean Bear reached our command he was killed, and fire opened upon his band. . . ."[28]

[25] *Ibid.,* 116.
[26] *Rebellion Records,* Series I, Vol. XXXIV, Part I, 935.
[27] *Rebellion Records,* Series I, Vol. XXXIV, Part IV, 151.
[28] "The Chivington Massacre," 75.
This agrees with Grinnell's account which quotes Wolf Chief, a participant, as a source: "A number of us mounted our horses and followed Lean Bear, the chief, out to meet the soldiers. We rode up on a hill and saw the soldiers coming in four groups with cannon drawn by horses. When we saw the soldiers all formed in line, we did not want to fight. Lean Bear, the chief, told us to stay behind him while he went forward to show his papers from Washington which would tell the soldiers we were friendly. The officer was in front of the line. Lean Bear had a medal on his breast given him at the time the Cheyennes

Major T. I. McKenny, special investigator for General Curtis who talked to members of Eayre's command shortly afterward at Fort Larned, made this report:

I have had several accounts of the battle or skirmish that took place between the Colorado troops and the Cheyennes. Fifteen wagons were purchased on the streets of Denver City, and Lieutenant Eayre, with two mountain howitzers and 84 men, all told, went in search of Indians, with instructions to burn bridges [villages] and kill Cheyennes whenever and wherever found. With his 84 men and only 15 wagons he wandered off out of his district, within 50 miles of this place. The Indians, finding his command well scattered, his wagons being behind without any rear guard, artillery in the center 1½ miles from them, and the cavalry 1 mile in advance, made an attack, killing 3 instantly and wounding 3 others, 1 dying two days afterward, the Colorado troops retreating to this

---

visited Washington in 1862 [1863]. He rode out to meet the officer, some of the Indians riding behind him. When they were twenty or thirty feet from the officer, he called out an order and the soldiers all fired together. Lean Bear and Star were shot, and fell from their ponies. As they lay on the ground the soldiers rode forward and shot them again." Grinnell, *The Fighting Cheyennes*, 145–46.

A soldier, Asbury Bird, gave this account: "The next morning, about 9 o'clock, we were attacked by about seven hundred Indians, and fought them until dark; we lost four men killed. We had no interpreter along with us. When the two Indians came to meet me they appeared friendly and ran off. No effort was made by Lieutenant Ayres to hold a talk with the Indians." "The Chivington Massacre," 72.

The site of this fight has been located at various places, but it was evidently close to the Smoky Hill some fifty miles northwest of Fort Larned. Squaw men Alfred Gay and John W. Smith were dispatched from Fort Cottonwood on June 2 to investigate into Cheyenne country. They reported that the Indians— 1,200 lodges of Cheyennes, Arapahoes, Comanches, Kiowas—were still in the vicinity, fifty miles north of Larned, and it was Eayre who had retreated from the field. According to Gay and Smith, only two Cheyenne chiefs and one brave were killed. *Rebellion Records*, Series I, Vol. XXXIV, Part IV, 460–62.

place. Lieutenant Burton, who was in the fight, is my authority. . . .[29]

Thus, in little over a month's time—April 12 to May 16—
Chivington's troops had had three major fights with the
Cheyennes, burned four of their villages, and killed a number
of their people including a head chief who prided himself on
his peaceful relations with the whites. The warriors of the
fighting Cheyenne tribe could no longer be held back by
Black Kettle and the other chiefs. Now the Cheyenne Dog
Soldiers and young warriors struck in retaliation, though it
was Kansas which suffered the main part of their vengeance.
In Colorado a few people blamed "old Chivington" for stirring
up an Indian war, but many followed Evans' theory that the
Cheyennes were working out a plot to run the whites out of
the country.

That fall the Commissioner of Indian Affairs, basing his
conclusions on reports from Evans, wrote, "From a careful
examination of them [accompanying papers, reports, and letters from Evans] I am unable to find any immediate cause
for the uprising of the Indian tribes of the plains, except the
active efforts upon their savage natures by the emissaries from
the hostile northern tribes."[30]

29 *Rebellion Records*, Series I, Vol. XXXIV, Part IV, 402–404.
30 *Annual Report* of the Commissioner of Indian Affairs, 1864, p. 167.

IV.

POLITICS
POLICY
AND PANIC

THE YEAR 1864 was a climactic and fateful one for Colorado Territory. The crisis impending between the whites and the Cheyennes and Arapahoes was abetted by a sense of foreboding which hung over the territory. News of Indian raids along the Platte route arrived daily in Denver, and North's story that the Sioux were uniting the tribes for a war against the whites quickly aroused the fear of another "Sioux Uprising" like the one in Minnesota. There in 1862 the Indians had revolted against the conduct of designing government agents and post traders in a general massacre which resulted in the killing of over seven hundred whites.[1]

The feeling of calamity was further magnified by natural

[1] According to Bull Bear it was the Yankton Sioux who were driven from Minnesota, along with the Missouri River Sioux, that had crossed the Platte in an attempt to stir up the southern tribes. "Sand Creek Massacre," 217.

disasters such as the Cherry Creek flood of May, which washed away a sizeable portion of Denver during the night, and a grasshopper plague of that summer which swept across Colorado like a storm front, devastating crops. To many Coloradans it looked as though even nature had allied herself against the whites and on the side of the Indian, who, in the wake of attacks by Dunn, Downing, and Eayre, were now striking blows of retaliation, mostly in Kansas but occasionally in Colorado.

Further, 1864 was a political year for the Territory, and, though it can never be accurately measured, the influence of this upon the Colorado leadership cannot be ignored. A statehood movement was underway, supported by Governor Evans and the Union Administration party which was running Chivington for congressman (representative) and Evans and Henry M. Teller for senators. A constitutional convention was held in Denver early in July, and an election was set for the second Tuesday in September. The issue of statehood was to be bitterly contested.[2]

In April (Eayre was still in Kansas, unheard from) Chivington informed Governor Evans that the threat of Confederate invasion on the southeastern border of the Territory would necessitate the concentration of troops there. He began moving companies of the Colorado First in that direction and suggested to Evans that a company of recruits be raised for the protection of Denver and the northern routes and settlements, recommending First Lieutenant George H. Stilwell be appointed recruiting officer and captain of the company.[3]

[2] Elmer Ellis, "Colorado's First Fight for Statehood 1865-1868," *The Colorado Magazine*, Vol. VIII (1931), 24-30.

[3] *Rebellion Records*, Series I, Vol. XXXIV, Part III, 335.

This was the inception of the Colorado Third Regiment of hundred-day volunteers.

From General Curtis, commanding the Department of Kansas at Fort Leavenworth, Chivington requested War Department authority to call out the Colorado militia in case of extreme necessity. The people, he said, would be terribly scared with no protection left them, though he himself did not believe that such protection would be necessary.[4]

At the same time Chivington requested permission from Curtis to take his Colorado First on a raid into Texas.[5] Curtis liked the idea and expressed his intentions of moving Chivington's force farther down the Arkansas for a summer campaign against the rebels.[6] Thus far the Indians had given little trouble either in Kansas or Colorado Territory, and neither man anticipated trouble from them.

Governor Evans, on the other hand, was taking the opposite view. He had been further warned by Gerry that the Cheyennes were angry over their recent troubles with the whites and had formed an alliance with the Kiowas and Comanches and "are now carrying out their hellish purposes according to their agreement." On May 28, Evans wrote to Curtis:

> That they are in strong force on the plains I have no doubt and if the U. S. troops are withdrawn I feel confident that they will wipe out our sparse settlements in spite of any home force we could muster against them. The troops have had several skirmishes with them, and at Cedar Cañon Major Downing gave a party of them a severe chastisement; but what has been done, the traders who know them well say, has only whetted their appetite for revenge, and has by no means subdued them.

[4] *Ibid.,* 354.
[5] *Ibid.*
[6] *Ibid.,* 406.

Unless a force can be sent out to chastise this combination severely and at once the delay will cost us a long and bloody war and the loss of a great many lives, with untold amounts of property. Our lines of communication, our main dependence for subsistence out here, will be plundered and the trains will be driven off the route in consequence of these dangers. The consequences to a people remote as we are from any supplies you can imagine for yourself, and I trust understand.

In the name of humanity, I ask that our troops now on the border of Kansas may not be taken away from us, just as they have been specially prepared to defend us by the Government and at the time of our greatest need of their services since the settlement of the country. . . .[7]

He followed this letter up a few days later with a complaint from a settler at Booneville who wanted protection from the Indians passing by his place on their way to raid the Utes.[8] The Indians, he claimed, had abused the women, killed cattle, and driven farmers from their land. Evans added to this his own impassioned cry again to keep the Colorado First at home.

"It will be destruction and death to Colorado," he wrote Curtis, "if our lines of communication are cut off, or if they are not kept so securely guarded as that freighters will not be afraid to cross the plains, especially by the Platte River, by which our subsistence comes."[9]

In response Curtis canceled his planned rendezvous with Chivington, ordering him to remain in Colorado. On June 13, Curtis wired Evans to act on his own authority in calling out the militia, adding that he hoped the federal troops in Colorado would be able to come forward soon.[10] Recruiting for the

[7] *Rebellion Records,* Series I, Vol. XXXIV, Part IV, 97–99.
[8] *Ibid.,* 206–208.
[9] *Ibid.,* 206.
[10] *Ibid.,* 353.

militia began immediately, but citizens showed scant interest in the program.

It was at this point that an event occurred near Denver which seemingly bore out everything that Evans had been saying. Thirty miles southeast of Denver a young ranchman, Ward Hungate, managed the ranch of Van Wormer. Hungate lived on the ranch with his wife and two children, a little girl of four and an infant. On the day of June 11, Hungate and a hired man named Miller were out looking for strayed stock when, from a high point, they looked back and saw the ranch house in flames. Fearing that Indians were to blame, Miller suggested that they ride to Denver for safety and help, but Hungate spurred his horse toward the ranch house to protect his family.

Accounts of the Hungate affair vary, but one of the more reliable is to be found in a letter written by three freighters who had left Denver on the morning of the twelfth upon hearing that forty to fifty mules belonging to them had been stampeded by Indians:

Ascertaining that the Indians, after taking a northeasterly direction, . . . had turned, and crossed the road near Box Elder Creek, we proceeded to that locality, and thence up that creek about 6 miles, where we met Mr. Johnson coming down, who imparted the startling intelligence that the family of a ranchman named Hungate, living a few miles farther up, had been brutally murdered by Indians, the ranch burned to the ground, and about 30 head of horses and mules driven off. The massacre had occurred on the day previous, some time shortly after noon, and Mr. Johnson had just assisted a party from the mill above in removing the bodies of the murdered woman and children. His statement was substantially as follows: The party from the mill and himself, upon reaching the place, had found it in ruins and the house burned to the ground. About 100 yards from the desolated ranch they discovered the body of the murdered woman and her two dead children, one of which was a little girl of four years and the other an infant. The woman had been stabbed in several places and scalped, and the body bore evidences of having been violated. The two children had their throats cut, their heads being nearly severed from their bodies. Up to this time the body of the man had not been found, but upon our return down the creek, on the opposite side, we found the body. It was horribly mutilated and the scalp torn off."[11]

The Hungates had been killed by a party of Northern Arapahoes, only four in number, headed north from a southern camp; but from all appearances the assault on the people of Colorado Territory by a unified effort of the tribes had begun. The bodies of the Hungate family were brought to Denver and there "placed in a box, side by side, the two children between their parents, and shown to the people from a shed where the City Hall now stands. Everybody saw the four, and anger and revenge mounted all day long as the people filed past or remained to talk over Indian outrages and means of protection and reprisal."[12]

The murders and the morbid display of the mutilated bodies touched off a feeling of panic that swelled through Denver and to the surrounding areas, causing people from outlying ranches and settlements to hurry into town. Chivington ordered Captain Davidson and a company of the First out in pursuit of the Indians who had committed the outrage with orders to: "Be not misled by the flying rumors, and do

[11] *Ibid.*, 353–54.

[12] Robert Claiborne Pitzer, *Three Frontiers, Memories and a Portrait of Henry Littleton Pitzer,* 162–63.

not keep your command out longer than there is prospect of success nor encumber your command with prisoner Indians."[13] On June 14, Evans went past Curtis to Secretary of War Stanton, wiring, "Indian hostilities on our settlements commenced, as per information given you last fall. One settlement devastated 25 miles east of here; murdered and scalped bodies brought in to-day [He neglected to say how many.]. Our troops near all gone. Can furnish 100-days' men, if authorized to do so, to fight Indians. Militia cannot be made useful unless in the U. S. service, to co-operate with troops. Shall I call a regiment of 100-days' men or muster into U. S. service the militia?"[14]

Two days later he wrote to Curtis again, enclosing statements by North and another squaw man named McGaa, who claimed that the Cheyennes were leaders in a plot to run the white man out of Colorado Territory by plundering and impoverishing them to the point that they would leave.[15] Curtis, however, still did not consider the situation quite as bad as it was put to be by Evans, who insisted, "I am quite sure that the Minnesota horrors have only been spared a re-enactment by the timely notice we have had of this hostile alliance . . ."[16]

A few days later another incident occurred in Denver which indicates the effect which the Hungate massacre had on the public. An excellent account of the affair is provided by a participant:

Two days after the Hungate massacre, just as the home guard were disbanding from drilling on East Fourteenth

[13] *Rebellion Records*, Series I, Vol. XXXIV, Part IV, 330.
[14] *Ibid.*, 381.
[15] *Ibid.*, 421–23.
[16] *Ibid.*, 512–13.

Street, a man on a foaming steed galloped through our streets crying, "Indians are coming; Indians are advancing on the town to burn and massacre. Hurry your wives and children to places of safety!" Following close after this rider came men, women and children, in wagons, ox carts, on horseback and on foot, all pale with fear. The news swept over the town like the wind. Women and children of East Denver were hurried to the mint; those of West Denver to the upper story of the Commissary building on Ferry Street.

In those two buildings women and children congregated in every stage of dress and undress. Some came arrayed in their best, having planned for an evening with friends. Some as they sprang from their beds; some carrying clothing in arms; others carrying valuables, but the majority had with them whatever they had found nearest when the alarm was sounded. The men patrolled the two buildings of refuge. My sister and I were in the Commissary building. Its iron shutters to windows and doors were bolted, and at the foot of the outside stairs by which we had climbed to the upper story, two men were stationed with axes to cut the stairs away on the first sight of the red devils. To intensify the excitement three women who had looked upon the Hungate remains described that horror. Some prayed, and some fled to the roof of the building to at least get away from the sight and sounds about them.

No Indians appeared, and when after midnight scouts returned from a fruitless search outside the city limits, many families returned to their homes. Others remained until the sun was high in the heavens. Few houses in the city had been locked that night and many were left with doors and windows open and lamps burned within. But so general was the belief in a fast approaching death, or a still worse fate, that no thieving was done.[17]

It was later learned that the panic had been created by a

[17] Susan Riley Ashley, "Reminiscences of Colorado in the Early 'Sixties," *The Colorado Magazine,* Vol. XIII (1936), 219–30.

frightened rancher who had been out looking for his cattle and had seen a group of shapes moving around in disorder. Thinking them to be Indians, he had rushed to his neighbors and friends to save them. The snowball became an avalanche. What the rancher had actually seen was a group of drivers of a freight train camped for the night. They may have been under the influence of firewater.

During the excitement a mob had tried to break into the military ordnance storeroom, demanding the issue of arms and ammunition. They were held off for a time, but when they threatened to tear down the building, the doors were opened and the mob crowded in and helped themselves.[18]

In order to combat the reported alliance of the tribes, Evans began putting into operation a plan designed to separate the friendly Indians from the others so that a vigorous war could be waged against hostiles. He directed Agent Colley at Lyon to arrange for feeding and support of all friendly Indians of the Cheyenne and Arapaho tribes. "The war is opened in earnest," he wrote, "and upon your efforts to keep quiet the friendly as a nucleus for peace will depend its duration to some extent at least."[19] On June 27 he issued a proclamation to "the friendly Indians of the Plains":

Agents, interpreters, and traders will inform the friendly Indians of the plains that some members of their tribes have gone to war with the white people. They steal stock and run it off, hoping to escape detection and punishment. In some instances they have attacked and killed soldiers and murdered peaceable citizens. For this the Great Father is angry, and will certainly hunt them out and punish them, but he does not

[18] *Rebellion Records*, Series I, Vol. XXXIV, Part IV, 449.
[19] *Rebellion Records*, Series I, Vol. XLI, Part I, 963–64.

want to injure those who remain friendly to the whites. He
desires to protect and take care of them. For this purpose I
direct that all friendly Indians keep away from those who are
at war, and go to places of safety. Friendly Arapahoes and
Cheyennes belonging on the Arkansas River will go to Major
Colley, U. S. Indian agent at Fort Lyon, who will give them
provisions, and show them a place of safety. Friendly Kiowas
and Comanches will go to Fort Larned, where they will be
cared for in the same way. Friendly Sioux will go to their agent
at Fort Laramie for directions. Friendly Arapahoes and Cheyennes of the Upper Platte will go to Camp Collins on the
Cache la Poudre, where they will be assigned a place of safety
and provisions will be given them.

The object of this is to prevent friendly Indians from being
killed through mistake. None but those who intend to be
friendly with the whites must come to these places. The families of those who have gone to war with the whites must be
kept from among the friendly Indians. The war on hostile
Indians will be continued until they are all effectually sub-
dued.[20]

On June 29, Evans directed a copy of the proclamation to
Colley, telling him to use every means, including the help of
John and Jack Smith and Bent, to get it to the Indians.[21] Then
on July 14 he sent $3,000 to Colley at Fort Lyon by Chivington
—who had been at Lyon at the time of the Hungate massacre
and false Indian scare and had hurried back to Denver—with
which to feed the friendly Cheyennes and Arapahoes under
their treaty of Fort Laramie stipulations.[22]

On July 18 news arrived in Denver that the Indians had

[20] *Ibid.*, 964.
[21] "The Chivington Massacre," 55.
[22] *Annual Report* of the Commissioner of Indian Affairs, 1864, p. 373. The
treaty of Fort Laramie annuity commitments were retained under the treaty
of Fort Wise.

raided Bijou Ranch and killed and scalped two men on the road at Beaver Creek. The *Rocky Mountain News* for the nineteenth reported that three men were killed and that Indians were spotted lurking in bluffs between Junction and Beaver Creek. The city was full of Indian rumors, and the *News* stated: "Indian depredations were subjects of universal discussion through town last evening. No two persons had precisely the same ideas about Indian character, vices, virtues, wrongs or revenges."[23]

During July and August, Colorado Territory was disturbed considerably by another event which aroused a multitude of rumors that the rebels were again marching on Colorado. From Fort Lyon came reports of what appeared to be a rebel plundering of a wagon train at Cimarron Crossing, east of Fort Lyon on the Arkansas. Readers of the *News* on July 29 read an account of a soldier from Lyon who told how two men of Company F had been assigned to follow the trail from where the train was attacked. They were led southward toward Texas across the Cimarron and beyond both Canadian rivers to the Red River, where they turned back. Later, however, they came onto another trail headed toward Colorado, made by a party of approximately two hundred men. They had followed this trail for a time, and then cut around it to warn Fort Lyon.[24]

The attack on the train at Cimarron Crossing on May 26 had been made by a party of twenty-two rebels under a former Coloradan, Jim Reynolds, who had escaped from Denver's prison in 1862. This group left Texas on April 11, 1864, by permission of General Cooper to enter Colorado and recruit

[23] P. 3.
[24] P. 3.

64

for the Confederate Army. Their venture, however, developed into more of a series of robberies and holdups than a recruiting effort. They robbed the train at Cimarron Crossing, taking, according to their count, about $1,800 in specie, about the same amount in greenbacks, and a number of mules. Dividing the money and mules among themselves, the party returned to Fort Belknap in Texas where they sent the money home.[25]

On June 12 the Reynolds gang again headed for Colorado, though now thirteen of the group refused to go along. These men, it is believed, headed for New Mexico instead. The nine remaining members entered the South Park area through Pueblo and Cañon City on July 24.[26] On the road to Fairplay the gang met, captured, and robbed Major H. H. de Mary, manager of the Phillips lode. Taking him with them, the gang continued on to a stage station just out of Fairplay on the road to Denver. Here they waited until the coach from Buckskin Joe arrived and robbed it, taking the driver, Abe Williamson, and the stage line owner, Billy McClellan, prisoners. They robbed McClellan of $400 in currency, a gold watch, and his gun. They then added insult to injury by taking the poke of Abe Williamson, who felt that a stage driver's personal effects should be beyond the reaches of outlawry. The booty from the stage was about $3,000, mostly in gold dust.

During the following week the gang raided along the mountain route between Fairplay and Denver while two posses of miners and a company of First Cavalry under Lieutenant Maynard searched for them. The soldiers were unsuccessful, but on the evening of July 30 a posse from the Swan

[25] *Rebellion Records*, Series I, Vol. XLI, Part II, 753–54.

[26] Kenneth E. Englert, "Raids by Reynolds," *1956 Brand Book of the Denver Westerners* 151–52.

and Snake River settlements spotted the Reynolds gang's campfire off the trail near Kenosha Pass. A gun battle followed, but darkness prevented its continuance and both groups retreated. The next morning, however, the posse returned and found one of the gang, Owen Singleterry, dead, shot through the breast. He was wearing a blue United States soldier's coat. All the horses and personal effects of the bandits were captured, except what the men had on them at the time of the attack.[27]

The Reynolds gang now dispersed. Tom Holliman, who had been on guard when the posse attacked, was captured between South Park and Cañon City, and on August 4 a large party of about seventy-five citizens left Fairplay in search of the guerrillas with Holliman, in chains, at their lead. Also getting in on the chase was a company of First Colorado Cavalry from Camp Fillmore under Lieutenant Shoup. Picking up two of the bandits' trail in the mountains above Cañon City, Shoup pursued them to the Arkansas River. The river being in flood stage, the two men had continued on downstream. Shoup followed, leaving behind Lieutenant Chase to sweep the country in that locality and leaving a detachment to watch the road at Beaver Creek. At Jerome Ranch, twenty-five miles below Cañon City, the two bandits being trailed by Shoup hastily constructed a log raft and crossed the river.[28]

On August 13, Shoup reported to Denver headquarters from Pueblo:

[27] Ibid., 164-65.

Singleterry's head was severed from his body and taken into Fairplay, where it was preserved in alcohol and displayed around the mining town for several years afterward. Ibid., 165-66.

[28] Ibid., 167-68 (quotes letter of Lieutenant Shoup written from Jerome Ranch on August 9).

Sir: I have the honor to inform you that the detachment of Company H, left at Beaver Creek, arrived here about noon to-day with three more of the robbers. They were taken this morning at Mr. Conley's ranch, on Beaver Creek, where they came in for breakfast. They were arrested by Mr. C[onley] and others just as they sat down to eat. . . . Lieutenant Chase has just arrived from twenty miles up the river; says he has two of the band corralled in a large bottom covered with all kinds of verdure. He had not men enough to watch all the avenues of escape and search at the same time; he therefore placed men on guard until more men can go up. We are determined to catch all of the rascals. I have all the roads and trails leading south so well guarded that I think it impossible for them to escape us.[29]

Eventually five of the gang were captured and taken, along with Holliman, to Denver by Shoup. Three of the rebels—John Reynolds, Jake Stowe, and John Andrews—were pursued by a company of Colorado First as far south as the Two Buttes near the New Mexico border, but they escaped.

Evans meanwhile continued his excited barrage of pressure upon Washington for authority to organize the hundred-day volunteers. On August 10 he wrote the Commissioner of Indian Affairs:

I am now satisfied that the tribes of the plains are nearly all combined in this terrible war, as apprehended last winter. It will be the largest Indian war this country ever had, extending from Texas to the British lines, involving nearly all the wild tribes of the plains. Please bring all the force of your department to bear in favor of speedy re-enforcement of our troops, and get me authority to raise a regiment of 100-days mounted

[29] *Rebellion Records*, Series I, Vol. XLI, Part II, p. 753–54.

men. Our militia law is inoperative, and unless this authority is given we will be destroyed.[30]

On the same date he wired Stanton: "The alliance of Indians on the plains reported last winter in my communication is now undoubted. A large force, say 10,000 troops, will be necessary to defend the lines and put down hostilities. Unless they can be sent at once we will be cut off and destroyed."[31]

Evans' plan to separate the friendly from the hostile Indians may very well have worked had it been given time, but on August 11, only forty-five days after issuing the first proclamation, he impatiently abandoned the plan and issued a second proclamation, this time to the people of Colorado Territory, without bothering to notify the Indians that his previous declaration promising friendly Indians safety had been voided:

PROCLAMATION

Having sent special messengers to the Indians of the plains, directing the friendly to rendezvous at Fort Lyon, Fort Larned, Fort Laramie, and Camp Collins for safety and protection, warning them that all hostile Indians would be pursued and destroyed, and the last of said messengers having now returned, and the evidence being conclusive that most of the Indian tribes of the plains are at war and hostile to the whites, and having to the utmost of my ability endeavored to induce all of the Indians of the plains to come to said places of rendezvous, promising them subsistence and protection, which, with a few exceptions, they have refused to do:

Now, therefore, I, John Evans, governor of Colorado Territory, do issue this my proclamation, authorizing all citizens of Colorado, either individually or in such parties as they may

[30] *Ibid.,* 644.
[31] *Ibid.*

organize, to go in pursuit of all hostile Indians on the plains, scrupulously avoiding those who have responded to my said call to rendezvous at the points indicated; also, to kill and destroy, as enemies of the country, wherever they may be found, all such hostile Indians. And further, as the only reward I am authorized to offer for such services, I hereby empower such citizens, or parties of citizens, to take captive, and hold to their own private use and benefit, all the property of said hostile Indians that they may capture, and to receive for all stolen property recovered from said Indians such reward as may be deemed proper and just therefor.

I further offer to all such parties as will organize under the militia law of the Territory for the purpose to furnish them arms and ammunition, and to present their accounts for pay as regular soldiers for themselves, their horses, their subsistence, and transportation, to Congress, under the assurance of the department commander that they will be paid.

The conflict is upon us, and all good citizens are called upon to do their duty for the defence of their homes and families.[32]

On the same day that his proclamation appeared in the *News,* August 11, Evans received dispatches from General Curtis and from the War Department authorizing the hundred-day volunteers' regiment. The militia was immediately transferred into the new Colorado Third Volunteer Regiment and on August 13, Evans wired Stanton, "Have 200 100-days men offered if they can be mounted and go at once. Indians reported near here and we are in great danger for want of

[32] "Massacre of Cheyenne Indians" in *Report of the Joint Committee on the Conduct of the War,* Part III, 47 (In subsequent references this document will be cited as "Massacre of Cheyenne Indians").

Evans personally dramatized the situation by going armed in the daytime, claiming it was the duty of every man to be able to defend himself at all times. "Nathaniel P. Hill Inspects Colorado. Letters Written in 1864," *The Colorado Magazine,* Vol. XXXIV (1957), 25.

troops. Please order quartermaster at Denver to mount and equip as fast as men enlist."[33]

On August 18 it was reported in Denver that a man and a boy had been killed by Indians on Running Creek south of Denver a few days past. Evans obviously used this as a basis for his exaggerated wire of the same date:

> Extensive Indian depredations with murder of families, oc-curred yesterday thirty miles south of Denver. Our lines of communication are cut, and our crops, our sole dependence, are all in exposed localities, and cannot be gathered by our scattered population. Large bodies of Indians are undoubtedly near to Denver, and we are in danger of destruction both from attacks of Indians and starvation. I earnestly request that Colonel Ford's regiment, Second Colorado Volunteers, be im-mediately sent to our relief. It is impossible to exaggerate our danger. We are doing all we can for our defense.[34]

He followed this up on August 22 with, "Unlimited infor-mation of contemplated attack by a large body of Indians in a few days along the entire line of our settlements. . . ."[35]

As a result of Evans' entreaties, Stanton ordered General Rosecrans, commanding the Department of the Missouri, to return the Second Colorado to the territory if he could possibly spare it. Rosecrans, however, could not do this immediately, and by the next month the Second Colorado was busy under Major General Pleasonton helping to defend Kansas City from the invading Confederate Army of General "Pap" Price.

The five members of the Reynolds gang who had been cap-tured by Shoup were placed in the United States prison in Denver, but Chivington, in the absence of the United States

33 *Rebellion Records,* Series I, Vol. XLI, Part II, 694.
34 *Ibid.,* 765.
35 *Ibid.,* 809.

Attorney in Colorado, S. E. Browne, convinced Hunt, the federal marshal, that it was in the power of the military to try the men by a military commission. Taking the prisoners into his custody, Chivington proceeded to appoint a military commission, which began taking testimony. On August 23 he wired headquarters at Leavenworth, "Have five notorious guerrillas. Will try by military commission. If convicted can I approve, and shoot them?"[36]

Curtis at that time being out on an Indian-hunting expedition in western Kansas, his Adjutant, Major S. S. Curtis, replied to Chivington. "The authority to confirm sentence of death is vested in the department commander. I do not think it can be delegated."[37]

This slowed Chivington down, but it did not stop him. Around the first of September the prisoners were turned over to Captain T. G. Cree of the newly-formed Third Regiment of the Colorado Volunteers, who left Denver with a large escort of troops to take the prisoners to Fort Lyon for trial. The 240 miles to Fort Lyon was a nine-day trip, but even so there were no rations drawn for the prisoners. Near Russellville, still in chains, the prisoners were shot "while attempting to escape."[38]

One account of this affair says that on the fourth morning out, the prisoners were taken several miles off the road and lined up for a firing squad by some of the troops, including Abe Williamson, the former stage driver, who was now a sergeant in the Third.[39] Jim Reynolds made a plea for their lives

[36] *Ibid.*, 828.
[37] *Ibid.*, 843.
[38] *Rebellion Records*, Series I, Vol. XLI, Part III, 596–97.
[39] George F. Willison, *Here They Dug The Gold* 148–53. Willison relies largely upon *Hands Up* by Dave Cook.

with Williamson on the grounds that when the situation was reversed they had not harmed him.

Williamson, however, showed no mercy and ordered his men back ten paces and gave the command to fire. But the newly-inducted soldiers had little stomach for playing firing squad, so that only Reynolds, who was opposite Williamson, was killed on the first fire. On the next order to fire, the troops threw down their guns, whereupon Williamson, infuriated, killed a second man. A sergeant named Shaw helped out and shot one man, but then he too weakened and Williamson killed the other two with a revolver.

It is for certain that the five men of the Reynolds gang, who had committed no crime worse than armed robbery in Colorado, were executed before reaching Lyon, and the indication is strong that Chivington was responsible. The *News's* version was that the prisoners were extremely abusive and insolent to Cree's soldiers and were killed to the man when they tried to make an escape.[40] Lieutenant Cramer of the Colorado First later testified that when he had met Captain Cree at Bent's Ranch, Cree had told him of killing some prisoners and that he had acted under orders of Chivington to "leave them on the prairie."[41] Cree testified that he told Cramer the prisoners had died "of want of breath" and claimed that he had taken it on his own to kill them.

United States Attorney Browne wrote to General Curtis of the matter:

... the whole five were butchered, and their bodies, with shackles on their legs, were left unburied on the plains, and yet

[40] *Rocky Mountain News,* September 9, 1864.
[41] "Sand Creek Massacre," 51, 191.

remain there unless devoured by the beasts of prey that don't wear shoulder-straps. Our people had no sympathy with these thieves, as they have none with other thieves, but they feel that our common manhood has been outraged, and demand that this foul murder shall not be sloughed over in quiet. When the news was first brought to Chivington of the death of these persons, and of the manner of their death, he sneeringly remarked to the bystanders: "I told the guard when they left that if they did not kill those fellows, I would play thunder with them." There is no doubt in the minds of our people that a most foul murder has been committed, and that, too, by the express order of old Chivington.[42]

[42] *Rebellion Records,* Series I, Vol. XLI, Part III, 596–97.

V.

FORAYS
ALONG THE
ARKANSAS

Fort Larned, Kansas, a collection of dirt-covered dugouts and huts, lay in a crook of the Pawnee Fork about ten miles from its juncture with the Arkansas. There were no walls of defense, only a few breastworks consisting of a short ditch with dirt piled in front of it. Larned was the jumping-off place for the long 240-mile trip to Fort Lyon along the desolate stretch of river which offered water, timber, and direction across an otherwise barren land. A large corral of horses was maintained at the post for the stage line and for the troops who rode escort on the difficult road from there to Lyon, the "Long Route," which was plagued by blistering, suffocating heat and dust in the summer months and by stinging winds and travel-killing blizzards in the winter.

Larned was a favorite gathering point for the tribes—Kiowas, Comanches, Cheyennes, Arapahoes, Plains Apaches, and sometimes the Osages and others—who found the post an attraction because of the annuities which were often issued there and because it was near the buffalo range. Jesse Crane, the Larned sutler, kept a large supply of whisky on hand, which the Indians either purchased with robes or through prostitution of their women to soldiers and other whites. The venereal disease rate was very high. In the evenings the Indians sometimes entertained the soldiers with dancing, or engaged in horse-racing contests. Generally, the light, tough Indian ponies won easily over the large army animals.

Lieutenant Eayre arrived at Fort Larned on May 17 and gave his version of his battle with the Indians to the commanding officer there, heavy-drinking Captain J. W. Parmetar, who reported to headquarters at Fort Riley that he believed the Cheyennes would soon commence hostilities against the whites. "With the garrison at my command it is impossible for me to render any assistance in the way of escorts, and, unless there is a cavalry force sent here, travel across the plains will have to be entirely suspended."[1]

The Cheyennes did not disappoint Parmetar, for on that very same day a war party descended upon the ranch of a man named Rath, thirty-two miles east of Fort Larned, driving off his stock plus some mules belonging to the stage station there.[2] The promiscuous killing of Lean Bear had exploded the wrath of the Dog Soldiers beyond the control of the chiefs, and this was the beginning of the Cheyenne uprising that was to continue through the summer of 1864.

It was Kansas which suffered the main portion of the Chey-

[1] *Rebellion Records*, Series I, Vol. XXXIV, Part III, 643.
[2] *Ibid.*, 661.

enne retaliatory raids, and a report made by H. L. Jones, dep-
uty United States marshal, gives a good picture of the havoc
wrought along the Big Bend of the Arkansas:

On Tuesday, the 17th of May, a man came in great haste
from the west to this place, having run down 2 horses in 40
miles, stating that the Indians had attacked the ranches on the
Fort Riley and Ford (*sic*) Larned road, killed some, and taken
the mail stock, and that they were coming toward the settlement. I immediately called the settlement together, and in a
few hours we were prepared for an attack.

Wednesday the stage drivers and ranch keepers came in and
partially confirmed the report. A man by the name of Walker,
at the Cow Creek ranch, who was tending stock for the Kansas
Stage Company, had been shot and the others fired at by the
Indians; the men from the ranch, however, driving them back,
killing 2 and wounding another. The men from the ranch then
fled, supposing that the Indians would soon be back with re-
enforcements.

The ranch keeper at Walnut also reported that they made
their appearance at his ranch, ordered him to leave instanter,
or he would be killed, and took away with them his wife, a
Cheyenne squaw. They told him that they had just had a fight
with the troops from Colorado on the Smoky Hill, that their
chief had been killed, and that they intended to kill all the
whites they could find, but being friendly toward him on account of his wife warned him to get out of the way. Upon receiving this news. I immediately dispatched a messenger to
Fort Riley for troops. Forty-five immediately started for our
place, arriving about midnight Thursday night. Friday morning, with 15 soldiers, under Lieutenant Van Antwerp and a
posse of citizens, I started west to search for the mail, which
was supposed to be on the road somewhere, and to bury the
man killed at Cow Creek. We found the man, the arrow still
sticking in his body, buried him, and proceeded on west with
the 15 soldiers in search of the mail.

We found all the ranches west of this deserted and sacked, but could find nothing of the mail till we reached Fort Larned, where we found it had not started, as the Colorado troops who had had the fight with the Indians had reached the fort in thirty-six or forty hours after the fight and reported the danger.

The commander of the post called a council of the Arapahoes, Kiowas, and Comanches who were about the fort, to know their intentions. They all professed themselves adverse to going to war, but none but the Comanches seemed to have any censure for the Cheyennes. They said the Sioux were with the Cheyennes and that 10 Sioux and 7 Cheyennes were killed in the fight; said the Indians claimed the victory and were still in the same vicinity where the fight occurred; admitted that they had asked them to join them. While they were thus nominally professing to be peaceable, they robbed a train of wagons within a few miles of the fort of all their provisions, and word came that they had just robbed a corn train on the road to Fort Lyon.

We started with the U. S. mail from Fort Larned on the 24th, and reached Salina in two days and a half without any difficulty, though we were watched by scouting parties of Indians all the way. The stage stock is all off the road for 100 miles and every station keeper has left.[3]

On June 3 the post office agent at Leavenworth complained to General Curtis of the Cheyenne disturbances and requested protection for the road between Forts Riley and Larned. As a result Curtis sent orders to both forts to protect the mails and trains with escorts,[4] a thing much more easily ordered than carried out. Deciding to gain a more direct report on the affairs with the Indians in western Kansas and concerning his forces there, Curtis dispatched his confidential staff officer,

[3] *Rebellion Records*, Series I, Vol. XXXIV, Part IV, 149–50.
[4] *Ibid.*, 205.

Major T. I. McKenny, to Fort Larned to investigate. Mc-
Kenny's report of June 15 is enlightening of the situation at
Larned:

> Arrived at Fort Larned on the evening of the 14th, during
> a very heavy thunder storm, and found the commander of the
> post with about half the garrison on a scout after Indians, but
> they got no Indians but plenty of buffalo. Captain Parmetar,
> of the Twelfth Kansas Infantry, in command here, is reported
> by every officer and man that I have heard speak of him as a
> confirmed drunkard. . . . In regard to these Indian difficulties,
> I think if great caution is not exercised on our part there will
> be a bloody war. It should be our policy to try and concilliate
> them, guard our mails and trains well to prevent theft, and
> stop these scouting parties that are roaming over the country
> who do not know one tribe from another and who will kill
> anything in the shape of an Indian. It will require but few
> murders on the part of our troops to unite all these warlike
> tribes of the plains, who have been at peace for years and inter-
> married amongst one another.[5]

The raids in Kansas would undoubtedly have reached even
more serious proportions had it not been for the efforts of the
white man who had known the Cheyennes the longest, William Bent. Bent, on his way to the States, had met Lieutenant
Eayre near Fort Lyon.[6] Eayre, having left his troops at Larned,
was proceeding on orders to Fort Lyon. After hearing Eayre's
report of the fight, Bent continued on his way, but before
reaching Larned he was intercepted by messengers from
Black Kettle who sent word of the battle with the white soldiers. The Cheyennes did not know what the fight was for,
and they wanted Bent to come out and talk to them about it.

[5] *Ibid.*, 402–404.
[6] "The Chivington Massacre," 93.

Bent sent word to Black Kettle that he would come, and seven days later met with the Cheyennes on Coon Creek.

After conferring with Black Kettle, Bent started for Fort Leavenworth, then changed his mind, deciding that he could do more good by talking with the Colorado authorities, and returned to Fort Lyon. His return to the fort coincided with the visit by Chivington. Bent told Chivington of his talk with Black Kettle and of the Cheyenne desire for peace but made little impression. Chivington stated that he was not authorized to make peace with the Indians and that he himself was then "on the warpath."

Bent tried to impress Chivington with the danger of a war with the tribes. He pointed out that there were a great many trains traveling to New Mexico and other points, also that there were citizens along the Arkansas trail who needed protection. Obviously there was not sufficient military force to protect the travel and the settlements from Indian raids. Chivington stubbornly replied that the citizens would have to protect themselves.

Seeing the futility of trying to reason with a man who knew nothing about the Indian situation, Bent left in exasperation and returned to his ranch. A week later he received a letter from Agent Colley, requesting him to come back to Fort Lyon. Bent complied, and Colley showed him the first proclamation to the Indians issued by Governor Evans accompanied by the Governor's letter ordering Colley to carry out the plan of the circular. Smith being unavailable, Colley requested that Bent go out to the various tribes and fetch them in to Lyon and Larned, promising that they should be protected by the government and that rations would be issued to them.

Bent rode out immediately, finding the Cheyennes, Arapahoes, Kiowas, Comanches, and some Apaches all in the vicinity of Fort Larned. The Cheyennes alone were at war, though they had tried to get the others to join them and the Kiowas were evidencing some hostility. Bent explained the Governor's proclamation to the Cheyenne chiefs, and they agreed to accompany him to Larned to talk with Parmetar. Parmetar and the chiefs talked briefly, both expressing satisfaction with the intent of the proclamation.

A short time later, in late July, the Kiowas decided to make a raid on the Fort Larned horse herd. They invited some of the Arapahoes to join them, but the Arapahoes declined. One evening the Kiowas under Satanta sent some of their women in to the fort to hold a dance and distract the attention of the soldiers. While the dance was in progress, a war party stampeded the post horse herd and the women disappeared into the night. A number of the animals lost to the Indians belonged to Colorado troops who arrived there with Eayre. During the fracas, Satanta shot and wounded a post sentinel.

Desirous of proving his friendship for the whites, Arapaho Chief Left Hand took twenty-five men to the fort and offered his services in fighting the Kiowas and recovering the stock. Left Hand advanced to within four hundred yards of the fort carrying a white flag. Here he met a soldier and sent him to the fort with his offer. But instead of having the offer accepted, Left Hand was fired upon by a howitzer, making the Arapaho chief run for his life.[7] Following this incident the young men

[7] "Sand Creek Massacre," 30.

Left Hand later told Colley: "I was not much mad; but my boys were mad, and I could not control them. But as for me, I will not fight the whites, and you cannot make me do it. You may imprison me or kill me; but I will not fight the whites." "Massacre of Cheyenne Indians," 31.

of the Arapaho tribe began joining in with the Cheyenne Dog Soldiers and the Kiowas in making raids on the whites.

Chivington, under orders from Curtis to get rid of "that drunken captain," arrived at Larned by coach shortly after the attack by Satanta, placing Parmetar under arrest and appointing Captain Backus of the First Colorado to replace him in command of the post.[8]

Fort Lyon, Colorado Territory, sat on the north bank of the Arkansas River, just down from the mouth of the Caddoe. When Sedgwick had built the fort in the fall of 1860, he had utilized the native red sandstone which jutted in abundance from the nearby hillsides. The fort was a rectangle of rock quarters, stuck together with clay mortar, with flat, dirt-covered roofs, and dirt floors. Facing each other from the east and west were two rows of soldiers' quarters, on the south near the river were the nine-foot-high stone corrals, on the north were officer's quarters, eight of them, and the sutler's store. There was also a hospital, bakehouse, laundry, guardhouse, and stage station. In the center of the compound stood the flagpole, a series of cottonwood poles lashed to one another. A bluff rose above the fort to the north, while to the south the river was landmarked by a grove of large cottonwood trees, known as the "Big Timbers" and called "Pretty Encampment" by the Indians.

[8] *Rocky Mountain News*, August 1, 1864.

Chivington took John Smith with him along the entire distance of the Arkansas from Fort Larned to Pueblo and "found him at home by night and day on the whole route." *Rebellion Records*, Series I, Vol. XLI, Part II, 660.

During this trip a band of Indians approached the stage but were driven off by the strong escort with an exchange of fire. According to Colley, the Indian band was accompanying Jack Smith, who wanted to see if John Smith were in the coach. "Massacre of Cheyenne Indians," 32.

Almost a mile to the east, on a rocky ledge which ran to the river's edge and broke off into a precipitous cliff, stood Bent's New Fort, built in 1853 and now serving as a commissary for Fort Lyon. It was well made of standstone and measured approximately one hundred by two hundred feet. Cacti lined the roof, and the muzzles of howitzers poked through portholes at the northeast and northwest corners. From here the eye could view the land as it lifted in barren, rolling hills and watch wagon trains grow small along the river. Some of the caravans would turn south through Raton Pass to Taos or Santa Fe, while others would continue on westward along the river to Pueblo, thence north to Denver and the Colorado gold fields, or through the Sangre de Cristo Pass to Fort Garland and on to Arizona and faraway California.

When Major Edward Wynkoop[9] arrived to take command

[9] Edward W. Wynkoop was a tall, good-looking young man, not yet twenty-six years of age in 1864, from a well-to-do Pennsylvania family. He had come west in 1856 with a yen to involve himself in as much as possible of the adventure to be had in the raw lands west of St. Louis. His first big chance came when he was appointed sheriff of Arapahoe County, Kansas Territory, which then extended into the Rocky Mountains, and joined a gold rush group to explore the region in the fall of 1858. Wynkoop was thus a member of the Leavenworth-Lecompton gold rush party, third major group to reach the mouth of Cherry Creek and the one which actually founded the settlement of Denver City. Wynkoop is credited by his son with having suggested the naming of the town after Governor Denver of Kansas Territory. That winter Wynkoop and a man named Al Steinberger trekked from Denver to Lecompton for the purpose of securing a charter for the Denver Town Company. The trip was made along the Platte trail, which was unknown to either of them, in freezing cold and across long stretches of unmarked plains. It was a heroic, if foolhardy, effort. Wynkoop returned in time for the first big strike. Taking up a claim on Clear Creek, northwest of Denver, he placer mined for a time, taking out a sizeable stake before selling his interest in the gulch. In December, Wynkoop ran for and was elected to the office of sheriff. When the Colorado First Regiment was formed, Wynkoop was appointed as captain of Company A, the *Rocky Mountain News* reporting: "Our military looking friend, Ned Wynkoop, stepped at once from Second Lieutenancy to a Captaincy of

COLORADO OFFICERS

Back row, standing, l. to r.: Captain Silas S. Soule, Captain
James M. Shaffer, Captain Samuel H. Cook; front row: Captain S. M. Robbins, Dr. John F. Hamilton, Major E. W. Wynkoop, Colonel James M. Ford.

INDIAN CHIEFS—1851

These three chiefs are identified as White Antelope, Man on a Cloud, and Roman Nose. Quite likely they are White Antelope, Man on a Cloud (Alights on a Cloud, He Who Moves on the Cloud) and Little Chief, Cheyennes, who visited Washington, D. C. with Fitzpatrick and John Smith in 1851.

Courtesy The Smithsonian Institution Bureau of American Ethnology

of Fort Lyon on May 9, 1864, he found the fort in a serious state of delapidation. Quarters were in desperate need of repair, and; because of the long absence of vegetables on the post, scurvy had broken out among the men, some of them being in serious condition and practically all being affected. Wynkoop immediately began repair work on the quarters and urgently requested vegetables from headquarters in Denver. This request was fulfilled later that month with a shipment of potatoes.

Wynkoop's primary responsibility, military-wise, was to provide right flank lookout for General Curtis at Leavenworth against Confederate attack. Accordingly, Wynkoop established scouting pickets down the Arkansas, sixty miles below Lyon on the river at Camp Wynkoop. Upon arriving at Lyon, Wynkoop had requested full and thorough instructions from Chivington as to the course of action he should adopt with the Indians, stating that at that time there were Cheyennes camped in the vicinity of the post but that he had no information as to their committing any depredations.[10] In a dispatch dated May 31, Chivington clearly outlined his policy "The Cheyennes will have to be soundly whipped before they will be quiet. If any of them are caught in your vicinity kill them, as that is the only way."[11]

---

his company; and we may remark, none are better fitted for their position, than is Ned for the one he now occupies." When the Coloradans met the Texans at Apache Canyon, Wynkoop's Company A was assigned as skirmishers along the mountainside to outflank the Confederates. Wynkoop and his company were on hand, also, when Chivington sent the miners from the Colorado gulches scrambling down the mountainside to capture the Confederate baggage train. When Chivington was appointed colonel, Wynkoop was moved up to the Major's position.

[10] *Rebellion Records*, Series I, Vol. XXXIV, Part III, 531–32.

[11] *Ibid.*, Part IV, 151.

In the middle of May rumors of a threatened raid from Texas reached Wynkoop, and he immediately ordered scouts out in the direction of the Red River to the south.[12] This scouting party returned after some ten days in the field without having found any sign of rebels. Still concerned, Wynkoop reported, "I will be as vigilant as possible . . . give them another taste of Pigeon's Ranch and Apache Canyon..."[13] and ordered Lieutenant Wilson at Camp Wynkoop to send vedettes out in the direction of northwestern Texas. On the same day Wilson sent word that a wagonmaster had reported the approach of a body of Texans toward the post.[14] This supposed party was the Reynolds gang who had captured the train at Cimarron Crossing, leading the Fort Lyon soldiers to suspect that a command with broken-down stock and transportation was in the area.[15]

Wynkoop immediately dispatched Captain Hardy with a command to scout sixty miles east of Lyon and made ready to "assume some responsibilities which I sincerely hope will meet with the approval of the colonel commanding."[16] These assumed responsibilities included sending orders to Lieutenant Colonel Tappan at Fort Garland to make a forced march to Lyon and dispatching Lieutenant Baldwin to Fort Garland after the two howitzers there.[17] Tappan, however, reported to Chivington, "Nothing is stated to enable me to conclude whether the circumstances are such as to justify a forced march or not. . . . Shall await further orders."[18]

12 *Ibid., Part III,* 630–31.
13 *Ibid.,* Part IV, 208.
14 *Ibid.*
15 *Ibid.,* 229.
16 *Ibid.,* 55–56.
17 *Ibid.,* 273.
18 *Ibid.,* 252.

Captain Hardy returned from his scout up the Arkansas with a report that at a point north of the Cimarron Crossing he found the train of wagons that had been attacked by a party of about thirty white men who reportedly had taken seventy head of mules, ten thousand dollars in money, harness, singletrees, fifth chains, and other property in an attack on May 26. The marauding party (the Reynolds gang) had left in a southwesterly direction toward Texas.[19] This increased rumors of an approaching force of Texans, and Wynkoop kept scouting parties out constantly.

On August 7 a Mexican train encamped seven miles from Lyon was attacked by a party of Kiowas. One Mexican was killed, and the Indians took sugar, coffee, and provisions.[20] Upon receiving a report of the affair, Wynkoop dispatched a messenger to Captain Gray at Camp Wynkoop with orders to cut off the retreat of the Indians. Simultaneously Wynkoop took to the field with eighty men—Company D under Soule, K under Quimby, and G under Baldwin. He crossed the Arkansas and headed in pursuit, but his course was changed by a dispatch received in the field from Bent to the effect that a party of Indians led by none less than Satanta himself had been there.[21]

Satanta's party had reportedly attacked a house below Bent's a few miles and killed a family name Rule, then attempted to burn their house. Upon investigation, however, Wynkoop found that the house had been defended by four men who had stood off fourteen "red devils" and killed one. After two nights in the saddle, Wynkoop's force returned to

[19] *Ibid.*, 576.
[20] *Rebellion Records,* Series I, Vol. XLI, Part II, 735.
[21] *Ibid.*, Part I, 231–32.

the post. Upon arriving he was informed of a report that four men had been killed in another attack near the Cimarron Crossing. Wynkoop reported to Chivington that he did not have enough men to attack Satanta's thousand or more warriors on the Cimarron since he could not safely take more than fifty men away from the post at one time.[22]

On August 7, William Bent wrote to Agent Colley concerning the visit by Satanta:

About 10 or 11 o'clock to-day four Kiowa Indians came in sight and finally came up. One of them was Satanta, or Sitting Bear, and one of them the Little Mountain, or Tohason's son. They said they were on a war party, and when they first left their camp that there was a very large party of them, and on the Cimarron they killed five whites, and the most of the party turned back from there. The Little Mountain's son says he was sent to me by his father to see if I could not make peace with the whites and them. I told him that I could not say anything on the subject to them until I saw some of the proper authorities. I then told them that I had heard that General Curtis was at Fort Larned, and that he was a big chief, and that he was the man that they would have to talk to. They asked me about you. I told you were at the fort. The Indians are all over the hill, and I am afraid they have killed old man Rule's folks. I think I will have to move from here soon. The women are alarmed, and I don't think it safe here. We will send this down after night, as we don't think it safe to send a man in daylight. The Little Mountain's son appeared to be very anxious for peace, but it may all be a suck-in.[23]

The first encounter with the Arapahoes by the Fort Lyon

[22] *Ibid.*

[23] Bent added, "I am not in a very good humor, as my old squaw ran off a few days ago . . . with Jo. Barraldo, as she liked him better than she did me! If I ever get sight of the young man it will go hard with him." *Ibid.,* Part II, 735.

soldiers occurred on August 11 when a minor skirmish took place near the mouth of Sand Creek. Ordnance Sergeant Kenyon had ridden out from Lyon in search of stray horses, and near the Sand Creek juncture he sighted a party of some fifteen Indians riding toward him.[24]

Actually the Indians were a group of Arapahoes under sub-chief Neva, who had been sent to Fort Lyon by Black Kettle with a letter for Major Colley which explained that the Indians did not want to fight and would not unless attacked. Neva had hallooed the soldier and waved the letter at him, and when he ran they gave chase.[25]

Kenyon, on the other hand, took the logical conclusion that these Indians were after his scalp. He made it safely into Lyon and reported the affair to Wynkoop, who put thirty troops in the saddle, divided into two squads under Lieutenants Cramer and Baldwin. Five miles east of Lyon, Cramer spotted the Indians and gave chase. After a pursuit of fifteen to twenty miles, he caught up with them, though a majority of the soldiers' horses had failed and fallen behind, there being only six troops with Cramer when he came up on the Indians. The Indians turned to charge but spotted the remainder of the soldiers coming up and again took off. A running fight fol-lowed, covering about four miles. The troops wounded four of the Indians, captured one pony, but failed to inflict any more serious damage because of failures of their Starr car-bines, of which only about two out of eleven would fire.[26]

Baldwin, meanwhile, had gone down the river with sixteen men and crossed twelve miles below the post. He was unsuc-

[24] *Ibid.*, Part I, 237–38.
[25] "Sand Creek Massacre," 33.
[26] *Rebellion Records,* Series I, Vol. XLI, Part I, 238–39.

cessful in locating Cramer, largely because of a rain squall which struck late in the evening, turning the night wet and cold. Since his men were poorly supplied with clothing and had no rations, Baldwin returned to the post.[27]

Upon receiving a report that Cramer was engaged with the Indians, Wynkoop dispatched Lieutenant Quimby with twenty men of Company K, but they likewise could not locate Cramer and returned.[28] Captain Gray arrived at Lyon with Company E in the meantime, and, leaving them to garrison the post, Wynkoop followed Quimby with Soule and a small detachment of troops. They, too, ran into the storm and were unable to locate Cramer, who had meanwhile come on in.[29]

On August 17, Captain Gray, stationed at Camp Fillmore near Boone's with thirty-eight men, investigated reports and found the dead bodies of three men on the river eight miles below the camp. He found also a government wagon and an ambulance containing some household furniture. Mrs. Julia S. Lambert, wife of the stationmaster at Fort Lyon, gives the most complete account of the incident:

A man named Snyder, who worked in the blacksmith shop [at Lyon], had sent east for his wife to come to Denver where he was to meet her and bring her to the fort. The quartermaster let him take a small ambulance, four mules and a driver for the trip.

He met her and came down to Pueblo, following that branch of the stage route. When they stopped at Booneville, twenty

[27] *Ibid.*, 239–40.
[28] *Ibid.*, 240.
[29] *Ibid.*, 237–38.
Neva later stated that his men wanted to come back and fight the soldiers during the rain storm but that he had been sent on a peace mission and did not wish to fight. "Sand Creek Massacre," 33.

miles east of Pueblo, Aunt Eliza, the old colored woman who had lived in Colonel Boone's family for many years, said, "You all got a mighty fine head of hair for the Injines to git, honey." This frightened and made her nervous and she replied, "Oh, don't say that, for I have heard such terrible stories of how they abuse the prisoners."

From there they travelled to Bent's Old Fort, where the stage from Santa Fe met the stage from Denver and consolidated, going to Fort Lyon which was thirty-five miles east.

The west-bound stage from Fort Lyon came upon the ambulance. The two men had been shot and scalped and the woman was gone. One of the wheel mules had been shot in order to stop the ambulance. The Indians had taken the other three. It was know there had been a woman in the party as articles belonging to her were found strewn around.[30]

The murders had been committed by an Arapaho party led by Little Raven's son.[31] They had also raided the agency on the day previous, taking twenty-eight head of stock, killing others, and during the same foray had dropped down to steal some horses from Charlie Autobees' ranch, south of the river.[32]

A week after these murders, on August 21, two men named Crawford and Hancock were massacred and scalped by Indians about eighteen miles west of Fort Lyon. These men had been on their way to Lyon to testify in the case of the government contractor, Haynes, before a military commission, and their bodies were found by a Fort Lyon civilian named Combs.[33]

[30] "Plain Tales of the Plains," *The Trail,* Vol. VIII (1916), No. 12, 8.

[31] "Sand Creek Massacre," 57, 216.

[32] Janet Lecompte, "Charles Autobees," *The Colorado Magazine,* Vol. XXXV, (1958), 303.

[33] *Annual Report* of the Commissioner of Indian Affairs, 1864, p. 375. Haynes was involved in stealing horses from Fort Lyon.

As a result of these murders, the Point of Rocks Agency was abandoned by the employees there, leaving what Colley estimated to be twenty thousand dollars worth of crops unprotected.[34] Colley also reported to Evans that the Arapahoes he had been feeding had not been in for a long time and it looked as though they might have to fight them all.[35] Wynkoop, in his reports to Chivington, declared, "My intention is to kill all Indians I may come across until I receive orders to the contrary from headquarters."[36]

[34] *Rebellion Records*, Series I, Vol. XLI, Part III, 122.
[35] *Annual Report* of the Commissioner of Indian Affairs, 1864, p. 375.
[36] *Rebellion Records*, Series I, Vol. XLI, Part I, 237–38.

VI.

INTO
INDIAN
COUNTRY

THE OUTBREAK OF HOSTILITIES of the summer and resultant depredations by Indians from the Platte to the Arkansas had brought a flood of complaints to Major General S. R. Curtis,[1] commanding the Department of Kansas. In July of 1864, Curtis arrived at Salina, Kansas, where he recruited a force of militia and volunteers for a movement against the Indians in western Kansas. In line with his plans, he created a new District of the Upper Arkansas and placed General Blunt in

[1] Curtis, an amiable and likeable graduate of West Point, had commanded the victorious forces at Pea Ridge, Arkansas, in March of 1862. For a time he was military commander in Missouri, but became so involved in the factional politics there that Lincoln was forced to remove him from command in that state. Albert Castel, "War and Politics: The Price Raid of 1864," *The Kansas Historical Quarterly*, Vol. XXIV (1958), 132.

command.[2] This new district encompassed Fort Lyon, removing that post from Chivington's District of Colorado. He also established Fort Zarah at the mouth of Walnut creek.

Before leaving Leavenworth, Curtis had dispatched a messenger to Wynkoop at Fort Lyon with orders to send four companies to meet him at Fort Larned. However, Wynkoop, remembering Chivington's orders not to send troops out of the district without his approval, forwarded the order-request to the Denver headquarters, thus delaying things for nearly two weeks. These Colorado First troops reached Larned on July 29, just as Curtis himself arrived there. Curtis was displeased over the delay and wrote to Chivington, "If instead of sending my orders to you from Lyon the commanding officer had moved promptly, a great portion of the murders and loss of stock that have occurred in this region would have been spared. I regret also that none of your field officers are here, although several of the companies are present with only two captains and very few lieutenants. . . . I fear your attention is too much attracted by other matters than your command. . . ."[3]

[2] *Rebellion Records*, Series I, Vol. XLI, Part II, 369.

James Blunt was born in 1826 in Maine, going to sea at the age of fifteen for five years. He later studied medicine, won a degree, and began practice in New Madison, Ohio. Moving to Kansas in 1856, Blunt became involved in the struggle against slavery and was drawn into the politics of the territory. When the Civil War began, he volunteered for service immediately and became Kansas' first major general. James G. Blunt, "General Blunt's Account of His Civil War Experiences," *The Kansas Historical Quarterly*, Vol. I (1932), 211.

[3] *Rebellion Records*, Series I, Vol. XLI, Part II, 483.

Chivington replied, "I assure you, general, that I have not spent an hour nor gone a mile to attend to other matters than my command." He explained that Anthony had been sick and would soon go to take command of Larned. *Ibid.*, 613–14.

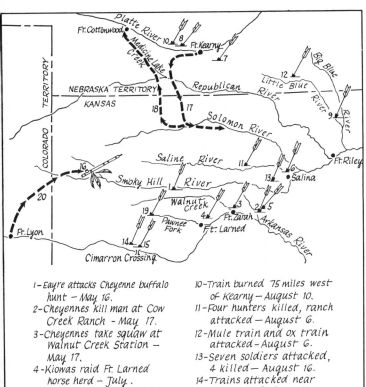

1 – Eayre attacks Cheyenne buffalo hunt – May 16.
2 – Cheyennes kill man at Cow Creek Ranch – May 17.
3 – Cheyennes take squaw at Walnut Creek Station – May 17.
4 – Kiowas raid Ft. Larned horse herd – July.
5 – Four trains besieged by Indians at Cow Creek – July 24.
6 – Indians steal horse herd at Salina – August 7.
7 – Trains attacked, 2 men killed east of Kearny – August 8.
8 – Trains attacked and burned, 14 men killed, 2 women and 4 children captured – Aug. 8.
9 – Little Blue settlements raided, 15 killed, Laura Roper and Mrs. Ewbanks captured – August 8.
10 – Train burned 75 miles west of Kearny – August 10.
11 – Four hunters killed, ranch attacked – August 6.
12 – Mule train and ox train attacked – August 6.
13 – Seven soldiers attacked, 4 killed – August 16.
14 – Trains attacked near Cimarron Springs, 10 men killed – August 19.
15 – Ninety-five wagon train attacked – August 21.
16 – Wynkoop parleys with Cheyennes – September 10.
17 – Curtis expedition – September 2 to September 13.
18 – Colonel Mitchell returns to Cottonwood Springs.
19 – Blunt and Anthony attack Cheyenne camp Sept. 25.
20 – Major Wynkoop's route to Smoky Hill.

The Cheyenne War of 1864
in Kansas and Nebraska Territory

Curtis remained in the field until early August without catching up with the Indians he was chasing, but contented himself in the belief that he had scared them away from the Santa Fe route. He hadn't. Curtis, in fact, had very little knowledge of the Plains Indians or how to fight them and later wrote to Blunt (who had little respect for Curtis) at Fort Riley that six hundred men and two mountain howitzers would be enough force to meet the combined forces of the Kiowas, Comanches, Arapahoes, Cheyennes, and Apaches.[4]

During August, 1864, the Indians struck throughout Kansas and Nebraska Territory. On August 6 a party of Indians caught four buffalo hunters on the Saline River, forty miles west of Salina, Kansas, and after a fierce fight killed the men and scalped them. They also made a descent upon a ranch house but were discouraged by an old man who shot one of them from a hole in the wall of the house.[5]

Governor Saunders of Nebraska Territory reported to Curtis that several trains had been attacked and destroyed in the Platte Valley just beyond Fort Kearny.[6] An ox train carrying machinery and a mule train loaded with merchandise for Salt Lake City were surrounded by Indians in early August between Atchison, Kansas, and Fort Kearny. The men in the mule train threw the goods out of their wagons, loaded up the crew of the ox train, and headed back for Atchison in a hurry.[7]

On August 23, Major Scott Anthony,[8] who had taken com-

[4] *Ibid.*, 629–30.

[5] *Ibid.*, 659–60.

[6] *Ibid.*, 643.

[7] *Ibid.*, 721–22.

[8] Like Wynkoop, Scott J. Anthony had taken part in the Kansas struggle. He had arrived in Kansas Territory in 1855 at the age of twenty-five and settled in Leavenworth as a partner in a merchandising firm. He was a cousin

mand of Fort Larned on August 13, reported to Curtis that the Indians had attacked a train near Cimarron Springs on the nineteenth, killing ten men and running off the train stock. The train had then been burned to the ground, and the victims horribly mutilated. To show their contempt for the whites, the Indians allowed a group of Mexicans to take a wagon and return to New Mexico.[9]

On August 21, some two hundred Indians attacked a group of trains, ninety-five wagons in all, sixty miles west of Larned. A wagon master was killed and a good deal of stock stolen. It was also reported that two men had been murdered between Larned and Lyon.[10]

Curtis had no sooner returned to his headquarters at Fort Leavenworth than reports came to him that Indian war parties had struck the settlements at the Narrows along the Little Blue River in northern Kansas, killing at least fifteen whites and taking captives.[11] Curtis immediately took off for Omaha

of Daniel R. Anthony, fiery Kansas newspaperman and of Susan B. Anthony, nationally-known leader of the woman's suffrage movement. When the Missouri proslavery raiders began harassing the Kansas towns, Anthony and twenty-six other men formed a vigilante group called the Leavenworth Rangers. In the spring of 1860, Anthony succumbed to the gold fever and the possibilities of trade in the mines. Outfitting with eight wagonloads of goods, he headed for California Gulch, now Leadville, where he and a partner opened a general store. On August 26, 1861, Anthony was appointed captain of Company E of the First Colorado Regiment. He and his company fought well during the New Mexico campaign.

[9] *Rebellion Records,* Series I, Vol. XLI, Part II, 827, 926.

[10] *Ibid.,* 827.

[11] *Ibid.,* 641–42.

On August 8, 1864, a Cheyenne war party attacked a frontier settlement on the Little Blue River in Kansas, robbing and burning the house of Mrs. Lucinda Ewbanks, a twenty-four-year-old woman with two children. Mrs. Ewbanks, the two children, ages three and one, her six-year-old nephew, and Laura Roper, seventeen, were taken prisoner. The Indians took them south

to look after Indian troubles in that region and to organize an expedition against the warring tribes. By September 2 he had gathered a small army of 628 troops, 76 of them Pawnee

---

across the Republican and west to a creek where they camped for a time. Shortly after the raid, the Indians took Mrs. Ewbanks' eldest girl from her and traded Mrs. Ewbanks to a Sioux named Two Face. He took her with his tribe which wandered that winter along the North Platte. During the winter the Cheyennes came to buy her back from Two Face, but the Sioux refused to give her up. Mrs. Ewbanks and her little daughter were recaptured on May 18, 1865, by white soldiers near Fort Laramie, and Two Face was hanged. Though her older daughter was saved by Wynkoop, Mrs. Ewbanks never saw her again for the child died in Denver in February of 1865. Her nephew also died at Denver. "The Chivington Massacre," 90–91; *Rebellion Records,* Series I, Vol. XLVIII, 276–77.

Mrs. Julia Lambert, wife of the stage line agent at Lyon, gave the following as Laura Roper's account of her capture: "I lived on the Blue River in Kansas. One Sunday I went to visit a neighbor Mrs. Eubanks, a short distance from my home. It was warm and a beautiful summer day. Late in the afternoon I spoke of returning home and Mr. and Mrs. Eubanks proposed accompanying me part of the way for a walk. She carried her baby in her arms and Mr. Eubanks was leading the little girl, who was about five years of age. We had to pass through a piece of timber and shortly after entering it we heard yelling behind us. We knew at once that it was Indians. The little girl began to cry and Mr. Eubanks took us off the road into the brush to hide. Not being able to quiet the child he stuffed his handkerchief into her mouth so tightly she could not cry out. We then kept very quiet until they had passed, yelling as only Indians can, expecting to overtake us soon.

"Mr. Eubanks had just taken the handkerchief out of the little girl's mouth when he heard them returning. The child screamed from fright and the Indians were upon us in an instant. They killed and scalped Mr. Eubanks before our eyes leaving his body where it fell.

"We were then put upon horses and our hands tied behind our backs. I had on a hat which an Indian took and put on his own head. He started off leading the horse I was on and headed off towards some of our neighbors. A woman lived in the first house who was simple minded. She was so crazed with fright when the Indians came that she tried to fight them, scratching and biting. They shot her and took her boy and another, each about nine years old with them. Bound on our horses so we were unable to move we had to witness these terrible things. They led my horse past the woman's body. She was not dead yet for as I passed she crossed her feet one over the other." "Plain Tales of the Plains," *The Trail,* Vol. VIII (1916), No. 12, 6.

Indian scouts, at Fort Kearny and begun his drive southward into Kansas.[12]

Curtis' luck had not improved; like Parmetar, he found plenty of buffalo but no Indians.[13] While in camp on the Solomon River around September 15, Curtis received a message that brought an abrupt conclusion to his Indian hunt. General Rosecrans, commanding the Department of the Missouri, notified him that a Confederate army under General Sterling "Pap" Price had crossed the Arkansas River and headed into Missouri. There was a chance he might turn into Kansas.[14]

On September 4, 1864, three Colorado First soldiers, on their way to Denver to muster out of the service, came across three Indians, two Cheyenne men and a woman, a short distance from Fort Lyon.[15] The soldiers were about to fire on the group when one of the Indians began making signs of peace and holding aloft a paper and pointing to it. Taking the Indians prisoner, the soldiers escorted them into Fort Lyon and notified Wynkoop, who reprimanded the soldiers for not following his standing orders to kill the Indians.[16]

John Smith was summoned, and Wynkoop began interrogation of the prisoners, who were identified as One-Eye, his wife, and a buck named Min-im-mie. Upon Wynkoop's

[12] *Rebellion Records,* Series I, Vol. XLI, Part III, 37.

[13] *Ibid.,* 180.

[14] *Ibid.*

[15] The following account of the trip to the Smoky Hill is taken from the testimonies and affidavits of Wynkoop, Soule, Cramer, and Smith found in the following documents: "Sand Creek Massacre," "Massacre of Cheyenne Indians," and "The Chivington Massacre."

[16] Edward W. Wynkoop's Unfinished Manuscript (Colorado History MSS II–20, Colorado State Historical Society), 27.

demand for an explanation of their coming to the post, One-Eye produced two letters, similar in content, one addressed to William Bent and the other to Major Colley. The letters had been written for them, One-Eye said, by George Bent,[17] who was now in the Cheyenne camp. The one to Colley read:

Cheyenne Village, August 29, 1864

We received a letter from Bent, wishing us to make peace. We held a council in regard to it; all came to the conclusion to make peace with you, providing you make peace with the Kiowas, Comanches, Arapahoes, Apaches, and Sioux. We are going to send a messenger to the Kiowas and to the other nations about our going to make peace with you. We heard that you have some prisoners at Denver; we have some prisoners of yours which we are willing to give up, providing you give up yours. There are three war parties out yet, and two of Arapahoes; they have been out some time and expected in soon. When we held this council there were a few Arapahoes and Sioux present. We want true news from you in return. (That is a letter.)

BLACK KETTLE and other Chiefs.[18]

One-Eye informed Wynkoop that there were about two thousand Cheyennes and Arapahoes, including about forty lodges of Sioux, congregated on the headwaters of the Smoky Hill River. The Indians wanted someone to come out there and have a talk to see if an understanding could be brought about between the Indians and the whites.

Wynkoop was suspicious that this might be nothing more than a ruse to lead himself and his men into a trap. He suggested that if such a trip were made, he would hold One-Eye

17 Edmund Guerrier stated that he wrote the letter with the help of George Bent. "The Chivington Massacre," 66.
18 "Sand Creek Massacre," 169.

and the others as hostages and would, at the first sign of treachery, kill them. One-Eye replied calmly that he was willing to die if the Cheyennes did not act in good faith toward the soldiers. The Cheyennes did not break their word, he said, and if they should he did not care to live longer anyway. He hoped, however, that they could leave for the Smoky Hill soon because he did not know how long the tribe would remain together.

Wynkoop was overwhelmingly impressed. "I was bewildered with an exhibition of such patriotism on the part of the two savages and felt myself in the presence of Superior beings; and these were the representatives of a race that I heretofore looked upon without exception as being cruel, treacherous, and blood-thirsty without feeling or affection for friend or kindred."[19]

The Cheyennes were willing to submit to arrest in the fort stockade while Wynkoop called a meeting of his officers in his room and debated the matter of taking an expedition to the Smoky Hill. With the presence of Captain Hill and his First New Mexico Volunteers,[20] it was possible to mount between 120–30 troops for such a venture, small numbers for a trip into the heart of Indian country. Despite the apparent sincerity of One-Eye and Min-im-mie, there were still good chances of a trap. On the other hand, for the oppor-

[19] Wynkoop's Unfinished MS, 28.

One-Eye, the father-in-law of rancher John Prowers, had been at Fort Lyon in July when Chivington was there. One-Eye wanted to go out to see the Indians but was afraid of the soldiers, and Chivington wrote a certificate of good character for him and told him to exhibit a white flag if he met any soldiers. "Massacre of Cheyenne Indians," 32.

[20] Wynkoop had requested assistance from General Carleton who commanded the military district of New Mexico. Carleton co-operated by ordering Captain Hill and a company of First New Mexico Volunteers to Fort Lyon.

tunity of rescuing the white prisoners alone, the risk seemed worthwhile. If the Indians were sincere in their claims for wanting peace, then countless lives might well be saved by meeting the Indians in council.

Two days later, on September 6, Wynkoop led a force of 127 mounted troops out of Fort Lyon, accompanied by John Smith and four Cheyenne prisoners—the three that had ridden in plus an Indian known as "The Fool," who had been living with a white man near the post. Two twelve-pound howitzers were taken along.

The expedition moved northeast toward the Smoky Hill, covering around thirty miles a day and crossing into Kansas on the third day. On the fourth day out, Wynkoop released Min-im-mie with instructions to contact the tribes and tell them that he had come in regard to the letter concerning the white prisoners. Early on the fifth day on a branch of the Smoky Hill (likely the North Fork), Wynkoop found his Indians, some five to eight hundred warriors drawn up in a line, making hostile demonstrations. It was an enormous and blood-chilling sight for the white troops.

Wynkoop immediately ordered his troops into a cavalry line of battle, forming his wagon train in a corral, and continued to advance. The movement excited the Indians even more, and they made ready to fight, moving their ponies into position and signaling to other Indians in the rear. They appeared to be well armed with bows and arrows and lances, and a great many had revolvers and rifles. Two hundred yards from them, Wynkoop halted his command and sent One-Eye forward with the same message he had given Min-im-mie, reminding the Cheyenne that his wife was still a hostage.

For a while it appeared that a fight was imminent, and that

the judgment of those who opposed this march had been correct. The soldiers were outnumbered at least five to one, and, if the Indians chose to fight, disaster was bound to result. The white men watched in anticipation as One-Eye rode out to meet the excited horde of Indians. One-Eye returned shortly, however, saying that Black Kettle had agreed to meet Wynkoop in council.

Wynkoop then fell back some eight miles with his force, trailed by a number of the Indians who kept up a howl. Some of the soldiers believed this to be their war song, but others claimed they were merely singing for grub. Wynkoop made camp on the bank of a dry creek, and at around nine o'clock on the morning of September 10, Black Kettle and his chiefs arrived to hold council with him. Present were all of the main chiefs of the Cheyenne and Arapaho tribes, who seated themselves in a circle of dusky, business-like faces, while Wynkoop, Soule, Cramer, and Phillips represented the whites. John Smith was helped in the interpreting by George Bent, who came with the chiefs from their camp.

The chiefs opened the council by asking Wynkoop why, if he wanted peace, had he come with soldiers and cannon. Wynkoop replied that while he had come in peace, he came ready to protect himself against bad Indians. He then produced the letter and read aloud the contents, asking the chiefs if it had been transmitted by their authority. They replied that it had. Wynkoop then stated that he did not wish to deceive them, that he was not a big enough chief to conclude the terms of peace, but that if they would deliver the white captives into his hands it would be the strongest guarantee that the Indians were earnest in their desires to live in amity with their white brothers. He further declared that if they would do this, he would do his utmost to help them and take them to a higher chief who could make peace. Wynkoop then read them the proclamation which Evans had directed to the Indians.[21]

Bull Bear, hulking leader of the Dog Soldiers, spoke first for the Indians. He said that he had tried to live in good faith with the white man, but a party of soldiers had come out and killed his brother, Lean Bear, who wanted to live in peace with the whites. He wound up his remarks by saying that he thought the Indians were not to blame for past troubles, that the whites were foxes (he might have meant "coyotes") and no peace could be brought about with them, and that the only thing the Indian could do was to fight.

Bull Bear's speech brought an excited murmur of talk through the group, but One-Eye stepped through the circle and demanded a chance to speak even though he was merely a subchief.

One-Eye stated that he had been sent into Fort Lyon with a letter, written by the chiefs, at the risk of his life, but that he was willing to run such a risk if, by so doing, he could bring about a peace or an understanding with the whites; that on his starting for Fort Lyon he had supposed that the chiefs were

21 "Sand Creek Massacre," p. 31.

Cramer testified: "He (Wynkoop) stated that he knew nothing about the whites holding any prisoners spoken of in the letter, and that if the authorities at Denver held any he could make no pledges to give them up; that he was acting upon his own responsibility and would pledge them nothing but what he knew he could fulfill, that chiefs bigger than he would have to decide that matter in Denver—that is, in relation to giving up the Indian prisoners; that what he had told them they could rely upon; that his life was a pledge for his words, and that the officers and men who were with him would sustain him. He then asked each officer in the council if he indorsed what had been said and the pledges that had been made, all replying that they did. The officers present were Captain S. S. Soule, Lieutenant Charles Phillips, Interpreter John Smith, and myself." *Ibid.*

acting in good faith, and that they would do as they had agreed, and believing that the Cheyennes did not lie, that he had offered himself to Major Wynkoop as a pledge of their good faith, so that if the Indians did not act in good faith his life should be forfeited, as he did not wish to live when Cheyennes broke their word; that he was ashamed to hear such talk in the council as that uttered by Bull Bear. He then appealed to the other chiefs to know if they would act like men and fulfill or live up to their word; that he had been sent by them to Fort Lyon and had taken their message to Major Wynkoop, (or their tall chief,) and that he believing them to be honest had come from Fort Lyon to talk with them; that he had pledged Major Wynkoop his word and his life, and the word of his, or their big chief, Black Kettle . . . and that he should stand by his word, (or fulfill his word,) and that if the chiefs did not act in good faith he should go with the whites and fight with them, and that he had a great many friends who would follow him.[22]

Left Hand spoke next. He said that his tribe had always been friendly with the whites and had had no trouble with them until the present season. He was particularly concerned with the recent difficulty between himself and the commanding officer at Fort Larned. He said that he had done all he could to prevent trouble, but that his men were fired upon when approaching the forts.

Next was Little Raven who took the floor briefly to indorse what had been said by Bull Bear. He stated that he had lived for several years among the whites and would like to shake

[22] *Ibid.*, 30–31. One-Eye went on to say that he was ashamed to hear chiefs get up, as Bull Bear had done, and make a fuss about a few horses and that he would be willing to divide the best stock he had with Bull Bear if he would have no more to say in council. Bull Bear accepted his proposition, took two of One-Eye's best horses and had no more to say.

hands with them, but was afraid that no peace could be brought about.

Throughout the entire proceedings Black Kettle had remained silent, sitting "calm, dignified, immovable with a slight smile upon his face."[23] He now arose, gathering his blanket about him. He said that he had sent One-Eye and Min-im-mie to Fort Lyon and had authorized the letter to be written. He was glad that it had resulted as it had in bringing Major Wynkoop out, and he was pleased to hear his brother chief, One-Eye, speak as he had. Cramer reported:

> Black Kettle, in his reply, said he was glad to hear his white brother talk; that he believed he was honest in what he said, and that he welcomed us as friends; that he believed that their troubles were over if they would follow the advice of the tall chief, meaning Major Wynkoop; that there were bad white men and bad Indians, and that the bad men on both sides had brought about this trouble; that some of his young men had joined in with them; that he was opposed to fighting and had done everything in his power to prevent it; that he believed that the blame rested with the whites; that they had commenced the war and forced the Indian to fight. He then gave an account of the first difficulties that occurred last winter and spring.[24]

The Cheyenne principal chief went on to say that so far as he was concerned he was willing to deliver up the white prisoners, knowing it was for the good of his people. But, he said, there were other chiefs who still felt unwilling to give up the prisoners simply on the promise of Wynkoop that he would

[23] Wynkoop's Unfinished MS, 29. This description of Black Kettle would also apply to the chief in the picture taken at Denver.

[24] "Sand Creek Massacre," 31–32.

endeavor to procure peace for them. These chiefs felt that the conditions of their giving up the captives should be an assurance of peace.

Wynkoop replied that he could only say what he had said before, that it was out of his power to make peace. He suggested that they considered his proposition among themselves. In the meantime he would march to a point twelve miles distant and camp two days, waiting for their word. He advised that they accede to his proposition as the best means of procuring the peace for which they were anxious.

Black Kettle agreed to this, saying that even if Wynkoop's suggestion was not accepted by the chiefs assembled, Wynkoop and his soldiers, who had come in good faith, would return to Fort Lyon unmolested. Black Kettle promised to be back at the required time, if possible, but since some of the prisoners were being held by the Sioux it might take some time to procure them.

While peace was being discussed in the council, a situation had been developing in the camp outside, threatening to explode the entire affair into bloody battle. Lieutenant Hardin, officer of the day, had been instructed by Wynkoop not to let the Indians, other than those in council, into the camp. But Hardin had found this order difficult to carry out, for all morning Indian bucks had been drifting in, poking with bland curiosity into the secrets of the white soldiers' camp.

One of the many fascinations for the Indians was the howitzers, and one brave tried to poke a grape into the vent of the field gun. He was immediately shoved back by the soldier guarding it. The guard drew his gun, and the Indian and his friends began making ready with their bows and arrows. The situation tanged like a bowstring throughout the camp. Excitedly, Hardin tried to line up his men in formation, and this only served to intensify the situation.

About this time Cramer left the council and arrived at the scene of the trouble. Sizing up the situation he wisely dismissed the men, instructing them to keep apart in groups just big enough to defend themselves, with a show of "reckless indifference" and to stay near the wagons which offered some protection. The matter was called to the attention of Black Kettle, who talked to his braves, and they began saddling their ponies and striking off.

The peace council ended around two o'clock that afternoon, and Wynkoop now moved his command some twelve miles back down the river, choosing a camp site of his own rather than the one which Black Kettle had suggested. Some of the soldiers, already nervous about the expedition, and now further excited by the episode with the Indians, began to talk mutiny. A group of them went to Wynkoop and demanded that he take them back to Fort Lyon, feeling that the Indians were about to betray them. Wynkoop talked with them, however, and told them exactly what had been said in the council, easing their fears somewhat.

It was at noon on the second day at this new camp that Wynkoop received word that a small Indian party was approaching. It was Left Hand, and with him was Laura Roper. Left Hand also carried a message from Black Kettle to the effect that he would make his appearance the next day, bringing with him the remaining captives. The Indians remained in the soldiers' camp as hostages.

Shortly after noon on the day following, a messenger arrived in camp informing Wynkoop that Black Kettle was near with the remaining captives. Wynkoop rode out to meet the

Cheyenne party and found that Black Kettle had with him three other white children. They were Daniel Marble, age seven or eight; Ambrose Archer, age seven or eight; and little Isabel Ewbanks (Eubanks), age four or five.[25]

Laura Roper told Wynkoop that Left Hand had promised before the Smoky Hill meeting that he would give her up if the whites would make a treaty. Black Kettle told of three other prisoners which he had not been able to get in as yet: Mrs. Ewbanks and her baby and a Mrs. Morton who was taken on the Platte. Mrs. Snyder had hanged herself.[26]

Wynkoop returned to Fort Lyon with the four captives, accompanied by all the Cheyenne and Arapaho principal chiefs, who had agreed to go with him to Denver to meet the Great Father and talk peace. The expedition had been an overwhelming success, and now Wynkoop looked hopefully forward to the journey to Denver and the securing of a solid peace for the Indians through Governor Evans.

At Fort Riley, in the meantime, General Blunt had been yearning to make a "pilgrimage" into the western part of his district and perhaps "steal a march on the red devils and give them a chastising, which is the only thing that will do them good—a little killing."[27] Anthony, also, had been wishing to conduct a campaign against the Indians. Finally on Septem-

[25] Ambrose Archer, Cramer stated, said he would just as lief stay with the Indians as not. *Ibid.*, 44.

[26] Julia Lambert quotes Laura Roper as saying: "I knew there were other white women in camp. One escaped only to be recaptured and brought back after a chase of some miles. During the night she took off her calico dress, tore the skirt into strips and twisted them into a rope with which she hung herself to the lodge poles. How she accomplished this no one knew as the poles are high in the center." *The Trail,* Vol. VIII (1916), No. 12, 7.

[27] *Rebellion Records,* Series I, Vol. XLI, Part II, 670–71.

ber 22 (while Wynkoop was on his way to Denver with the
Cheyenne and Arapaho chiefs) Blunt left Fort Larned with
four hundred men, provided with ten days' rations of hard
bread and half that amount of bacon, and two mountain howitzers. His intentions were to go south of the Arkansas toward
Crooked Creek and the Cimarron. The Delaware, Fall Leaf,
and some of his braves were scouting for him.[28]

After a two days' march, covering close to sixty miles on
the Wet Route of the Santa Fe road, Blunt reached the Cimarron Crossing of the Arkansas where he learned that a large
party of Indians were camped north of there on the Dry
branch of the road. Turning abruptly northward, Blunt's force
reached a point within eight or ten miles of the Pawnee Fork
on the evening of September 24 and went into camp. At three
o'clock the following morning, Blunt broke camp and continued northward, reaching the mouth of the Pawnee just as
the land was growing light. He then halted his force and sent
a scouting party up the creek in search of a crossing.

The scouts returned shortly and reported they had discovered an Indian lodge and some ponies about half a mile
up the fork. Blunt immediately sent out a small force to re-
connoiter up the river, and soon firing was heard from that
direction. Anthony, with fifty-nine men of Companies L and
M of the First Colorado Regiment, was then directed to rein-
force the scouts.

Blunt waited for an hour and upon hearing nothing from
Anthony moved upstream to support him. About a mile up
the river he discovered that Anthony's force, which had

[28] *Rebellion Records*, Series I, Vol. XLI, Part I, 818; "Massacre of Cheyenne Indians," 26. Fall Leaf was a famous scout of the time, having been with
Sumner during the 1856 campaign.

plunged headlong after what he thought to be a few Indians, was surrounded and was trying to fight his way back to Blunt. He had sent messengers out, but they had been cut off by the Indians. When Blunt came up, the Indians quickly retreated and disappeared toward the Smoky Hill.

The Indian camp had been a large one, situated ten miles up the Pawnee, and the Indians had been fighting their standard strategy—delay the enemy until the village can escape. Blunt pursued them for two days until his stock, inferior to that of the Indians, became exhausted and subsistence ran low, there being no game in the region.

The troops found nine dead Indians on the battlefield and surmised that more were killed, several having been seen to fall and be dragged from the field by their comrades. The whites' loss was one man killed and seven wounded.

This affair under his belt, Blunt was called to help Curtis contain the invading army of Price, which had cut westward into Kansas.

The Plains Indian war during the summer of 1864 thus accomplished what the Confederates had long hoped for—a general outbreak against the settlements and wagon routes in Kansas, Nebraska, and Colorado. When Price's attack came, it caught Curtis with his attention diverted to the Indian crisis. Fortunately for Curtis, and for the Union, Price arrived in Kansas too late and with too little. Otherwise the nation might have had even more cause to wonder just how the Indian War of 1864 had come about.

VII.

COUNCIL
AT
CAMP WELD

On September 18, 1864, Wynkoop wrote to Governor Evans concerning the Smoky Hill expedition, his meeting with the Indians, and the position he had taken, stating that he was starting immediately for Denver with the chiefs.[1] The peace caravan consisted of the four white captives, seven of the main chiefs of the Cheyenne and Arapaho tribes, Wynkoop, Soule, the son of Major Colley—D. D. Colley, John Smith, and an escort of forty soldiers under the command of Cramer. Representing the Cheyennes were Black Kettle, White Antelope, and Bull Bear. Little Raven and Left Hand remained behind, sending in their stead Neva, Bosse, Heaps-of-Buffalo, and No-ta-nee—all relatives of Left Hand.[2]

[1] "Sand Creek Massacre," 119–20.
[2] *Ibid.*, 86, 213.

At Booneville, Wynkoop left the caravan and rode ahead to Denver with the white captives and Dexter Colley, arriving there two days in advance of the rest, for the purpose of talking with Evans before the chiefs arrived. When he tried to contact Evans, however, he was informed that the Governor was sick in bed and could not see anyone. But the next morning Evans arrived at Wynkoop's hotel and the two men, with Dexter Colley present, had a lengthy conversation regarding the Indian situation.[3]

Wynkoop told Evans that the chiefs would be in Denver in a couple of days for the purpose of holding a council with him. According to Wynkoop, Evans was extremely displeased about the whole thing. He could have nothing to do with them, Evans said. They had declared war against the United States, and he considered them as being in the hands of the military authorities. Besides, it would not be good policy to make peace with the Cheyenne and Arapaho tribes until they were properly punished. Otherwise, he said, it would look as though the United States considered itself whipped.

Wynkoop replied that it would seem very strange to him that the United States should consider itself whipped by a few Indians, and called attention to the fact that he, as a United States officer, had brought these Indians over four hundred miles for the purpose of having an audience with the Governor and in answer to his proclamation. Evans still refused to hold the council, stating that he was due to leave the next day to visit the Ute agency in line with his position as ex-officio superintendent of Indian affairs in Colorado. Wynkoop testified that when he insisted further, Evans brought out what was probably his real reason for not wanting to talk

[3] *Ibid.*, 90; "The Chivington Massacre," 77.

111

peace with the Indians—the Colorado Third had been raised and equipped on the basis of his representations to Washington that the unit was needed to fight hostile Indians then ravaging the country. If he made peace with the Indians, it would appear to Washington that he had misrepresented matters and put the government to useless expense and trouble.[4]

On September 26, Chivington wired to Curtis at Leavenworth as follows:

I have been informed by E. W. Wynkoop, commanding Fort Lyon, that he is on his way here with Cheyenne and Arapaho chiefs and four white prisoners they gave up. Winter approaches. Third Regiment is full, and they know they will be chastised for their outrages and now want peace. I hope that the major-general will direct that they make full restitution and then go on their reserve and stay there.[5]

On the twenty-eighth, knowing but scant of the situation and following the lead suggested by Chivington's telegram, Curtis answered:

I shall require the bad Indians delivered up; restoration of equal numbers of stock; also hostages to secure. I want no peace till the Indians suffer more. Left Hand is said to be a good chief of the Arapahoes, but Big Mouth [whom Curtis hadn't been able to catch on the Arkansas] is a rascal. I fear agent of Interior Department will be ready to make presents too soon. It is better to chastise before giving anything but a little tobacco to talk over. No peace must be made without my directions.[6]

[4] "The Chivington Massacre," 77. In this affidavit Wynkoop stated, "Several times in our conversation in regard to the object of the Indians who were coming to see him, he made the remark, 'What shall I do with the third regiment, if I make peace?' "

[5] *Rebellion Records*, Series I, Vol. XLI, Part III, 399.

Evans could hardly avoid at least talking to the Indians, and eventually he gave in. Denver, meanwhile, had learned the news of the forthcoming visit by the Indian chiefs, and the town was strongly split on the situation, emotions running high. A large reception of carriages greeted the chiefs when they arrived cramped and stiff from the long ride in the crowded wagon.

On September 28 a council was held at Camp Weld, Evans presiding. In attendance were Wynkoop, Soule, Cramer, Chivington, Shoup, several other officers, John Smith, a Denver attorney named Amos Steck, Ute Agent Simeon Whiteley, plus several of the city's more prominent citizens. Before the meeting got under way, Evans requested that Whiteley make a record of the proceedings, warning him that "upon the results of this council very likely depended a continuance of the Indian war on the plains, and it was important that the minutes should be full and complete."[7] Whiteley frequently stopped the interview so that he could get every word down. John Smith interpreted.

Evans began the council by asking the chiefs what they had to say. Black Kettle was the first chief to rise from his position on the floor and speak for the Indians. His first words were to remind Evans that he had received the Governor's circular of June 27, saying that it had taken him some time after Bent had brought it out to get all his people together and hold a council in regard to it. After pointing out that the Cheyennes had complied with the terms of the circular by delivering up

---

[6] *Ibid.*, 462.

[7] "Sand Creek Massacre," 213.

The following account of the council at Camp Weld is based strictly upon the verbatim record of the conversation made by Whiteley. *Ibid.*, 213–17.

their prisoners and following Wynkoop to Fort Lyon, Black Kettle spoke with the picturesque eloquence typical of the American Indian:

> I followed Major Wynkoop to Fort Lyon, and Major Wynkoop proposed that we come up to see you. We have come with our eyes shut, following his handful of men, like coming through the fire. All we ask is that we may have peace with the whites; we want to hold you by the hand [to shake hands]. You are our father; we have been travelling through a cloud; the sky has been dark ever since the war began. These braves who are with me are all willing to do what I say. We want to take good tidings home to our people, that they may sleep in peace. I want you to give all the chiefs of the soldiers here to understand that we are for peace, and that we have made peace, that we may not be mistaken by them for enemies. I have not come with a little wolf's bark, but have come to talk plain with you. We must live near the buffalo or starve. When we came here we came free, without any apprehension, to see you, and when I go home and tell my people that I have taken your hand and the hands of all the chiefs here in Denver, they will feel well, and so will all the different tribes of Indians on the plains, after we have eaten and drunk with them.[8]

Evans, however, made little effort in the direction of peace. He accused the Cheyennes and Arapahoes of making an alliance with the Sioux, a point on which he had been misinformed. He further stated that while the government had been spending thousands of dollars in opening farms and making preparation to feed the Indians, they had joined in a war against the white man.

Governor Evans, (resuming.) I was under the necessity,

[8] *Ibid.,* 213.

Sketch made in 1863. The sutler's store to the far left is standing in this sketch while in the photograph below it appears
in ruins. The Indian lodges, curiously, are in much the same
position in both views.

Fort Lyon (Old), Colorado Territory

This remarkable photograph was taken from the Bent's Fort
bluff before the flood of 1866, which destroyed the stone corrals to the left. The presence of the Indians suggests that it
predates the Sand Creek Massacre.

ARRIVAL OF CHIEFS IN DENVER — 1864
The arrival of the Cheyenne and Arapaho chiefs and white
prisoners in Denver, September 28, 1864.

Courtesy Library, State Historical Society of Colorado

after all the trouble and expense I was at, of returning home without seeing them. Instead of this, your people went away and smoked the "war pipe" with our enemies.

Black Kettle. I don't know who could have told you this.

Governor Evans. No matter who said this, but your conduct has proved to my satisfaction that such was the case.[9]

This time several of the Indians spoke up to insist that this was not true, that they had made no alliance with the Sioux or anyone else. Evans explained that by "smoking the war pipe" he was speaking figuratively, but that their conduct had been such as to show they had an understanding with other tribes. The chiefs agreed that it may have appeared so. The Governor then went on to tell them that he was not interested in making peace now, that soon the "plains would swarm with United States soldiers." He said that he feared the chiefs could not control their people in holding to a peace except in the winter months, and then when the grass was green again they would go back to warring. Also, he stated, he had learned that the Indians thought they could drive the white man from the country, but soon the war with the rebel whites would be over and the Great Father would have enough soldiers to drive all the Indians from the Plains. He then reiterated the terms of his June proclamation, saying that his advice to them was to turn to the side of the government and show by acts their friendly disposition.

One of the Indians inquired as to what it meant to be on the side of the government. This was explained to mean that the Indians must obey the requirements of the military officers, to render them such assistance as they could by giving information, acting as scouts, and so forth. The chiefs all gave their

[9] *Ibid.*, 214.

consent to this, and Black Kettle replied, "We will return with Major Wynkoop to Fort Lyon; we will then proceed to our village and take back to my young men every word you say. I cannot answer for all of them, but think there will be little difficulty in getting them to assent to help the soldiers."[10]

Evans explained that if the Indians did not keep peace with the United States, or have an arrangement with them, they would be treated as enemies. At this point White Antelope took the floor:

> *White Antelope.* I understand every word you have said, and will hold on to it. I will give you an answer directly. The Cheyennes, all of them, have their ears open this way, and they will hear what you say. I am proud to have seen the chief of all the whites in this country. I will tell my people. Ever since I went to Washington [in 1851] and received this medal, I have called all white men as my brothers, but other Indians have since been to Washington and got medals, and now the soldiers do not shake hands, but seek to kill me. What do you mean by us fighting your enemies? Who are they?
>
> *Governor Evans.* All Indians who are fighting us.
>
> *White Antelope.* How can we be protected from the soldiers on the plains?
>
> *Governor Evans.* You must make that arrangement with the military chief.

[10] *Ibid.*, 215. Evans passed fleetingly over the key to the solution of the troubles with these tribes—the using of their warriors to fight on the side of the whites. It was virtually impossible that the young men could give up their heritage of war overnight. But given a chance to fight on the side of the whites against other tribes, they would have provided sorely-needed frontier troops, as Wynkoop pointed out to Curtis. Instead, the government would later utilize the Pawnees in this fashion under the North brothers to fight the Cheyennes. Many years later during the Nez Percés outbreak of 1877, the Cheyennes were used on the side of the whites. But by then the Cheyenne Nation was practically destroyed.

White Antelope. I fear these new soldiers who have gone out may kill some of my people while I am here.

Governor Evans. There is great danger of it.

White Antelope. When we sent our letter to Major Wynkoop, it was like going through a strong fire, or blast, for Major Wynkoop's men to come to our camp; it was the same for us to come to see you. We have our doubts whether the Indians south of the Arkansas, or those north of the Platte, will do as you say. A large number of Sioux have crossed the Platte in the vicinity of the Junction, into our country. When Major Wynkoop came, we proposed to make peace. He said he had no power to make peace, except to bring us here and return us safe.

Governor Evans, again. Whatever peace you make must be with the soldiers, and not with me. Are the Apaches at war with the whites?

White Antelope. Yes; and the Comanches and Kiowas, as well; also a tribe of Indians from Texas whose name we do not know. There are thirteen different bands of Sioux who have crossed the Platte, and are in alliance with the others named.

Governor Evans. How many warriors with the Apaches, Kiowas, and Comanches?

White Antelope. A good many; don't know.

Governor Evans. How many of the Sioux?

White Antelope. Don't know, but many more than the southern tribes.[11]

Evans now began to quiz the chiefs concerning recent conflicts between the Indians and whites:

Governor Evans. Who committed the depredations on the trains near the Junction, about the first of August?

White Antelope. Do not know; did not know any was committed; have taken you by the hand, and will tell the truth, keeping back nothing.

[11] *Ibid.,* 215.

Governor Evans. Who committed the murder of the Hunsgate [*sic*] family on Burning creek?

Neva. The Arapahoes, a party of the northern band who were passing north; it was Medicine Man, or Roman Nose, and three others.

Agent Whiteley. That cannot be true; I am satisfied, from the time he left a certain camp for the north, that it was not this party of four persons.

Governor Evans. Where is Roman Nose now?

Neva. You ought to know better than me; you have been nearer to him.

Governor Evans. Who killed a man and boy at the head of Cherry creek, four weeks ago?

Neva (*after consultation,*) Kiowas and Comanches.

Governor Evans. Who stole soldiers' horses and mules from Jimmie's camp, twenty-seven days ago?

Neva. Fourteen Cheyennes and Arapahoes together.

Governor Evans. What were their names?

Neva. Powder-face and Whirlwind, who are now in our camp, were the leaders.

Colonel Shoup. I counted twenty Indians on that occasion.

Governor Evans. Who stole Charley Antobe's horses?

Neva. Raven's son.

Governor Evans. Who took the stock from Fremont's Orchard, and had the first battle with the soldiers this spring, north of there?

White Antelope. Before answering this question, I would like for you to know that this was the beginning of the war, and I should like to know what it was for—a soldier fired first.

Governor Evans. The Indians had stolen about forty horses; the soldiers went to recover them, and the Indians fired a volley into their ranks.

White Antelope. This is all a mistake; they were coming down the Bijou, and found one horse and one mule. They returned one horse, before they got to Geary's, to a man; then went to Geary's, expecting to turn the other one over to some one. They then heard that the soldiers and the Indians were fighting somewhere down the Platte; they then took a fright, and all fled.

Governor Evans. Who were the Indians who had the fight?

White Antelope. They were headed by Fool Badger's son, a young man, one of the greatest of the Cheyenne warriors, who was wounded, and, though still alive, he will never recover.

Neva. I want to say something. It makes me feel bad to be talking about these things, and opening old sores.

Governor Evans. Let him speak.

Neva. Mr. Smith has known me ever since I was a child; has he ever known me commit depredations on the whites? I went to Washington last year, receiving good counsel; I hold on to it. I am determined always to keep peace with the whites. Now, when I shake hands with them they seem to pull away. I came here to seek peace, and nothing else.

Governor Evans. We feel that you have, by your stealing and murdering, done us great damage. You come here and say you will tell us all, and that is what I am trying to get.

Neva. The Comanches, Kiowas, and Sioux have done much more injury than we have. We will tell you what we know, but cannot answer for others.

Governor Evans. I suppose you acknowledge the depredations on the Little Blue, as you have the prisoners there taken in your possession?

White Antelope. We (the Cheyennes) took two prisoners west of Fort Kearney, and destroyed the trains.

Governor Evans. Who committed depredations at Cottonwood?

White Antelope. The Sioux; what band I do not know.

Governor Evans. What are the Sioux going to do next?

Bull Bear. Their intention is to clear out all this country. They are angry, and will do all the damage to the whites they can. I am with you and the troops to fight all those who have no ears to listen to what you say. Who are they? Show them to

me—I am young. I have never harmed a white man. I am push-
ing for something good. I am always going to be friendly with
the whites; they can do me good.

Governor Evans. Where are those Sioux?

Bull Bear. Down on the Republican, where it opens out.

Governor Evans. Do you know that they intend to attack
the trains this week?

Bull Bear. Yes; about one-half of all the Missouri river Sioux
and Yanktons who were driven from Minnesota are those who
have crossed the Platte. I am young, and can fight. I have
given my word to fight with the whites. My brother, Lean
Bear, died in trying to keep peace with the whites. I am willing to die in the same way, and expect to do so.

Neva. I know the value of the presents which we receive
from Washington; we cannot live without them. That is why
I try so hard to keep peace with the whites.[12]

It was at this point that Chivington took the floor to have
his only say during the council:

Colonel Chivington. I am not a big war chief, but all the
soldiers in this country are at my command. My rule of fighting white men or Indians is, to fight them until they lay down
their arms and submit to military authority. You are nearer
Major Wynkoop than any one else, and you can go to him
when you get ready to do that.[13]

With this the council adjourned. The chiefs were happy
with the meeting and shook hands all around.[14] Black Kettle
embraced Governor Evans and Major Wynkoop. After the
meeting, the Indians consented to having their pictures taken,

[12] *Ibid.*, 215–17.

[13] *Ibid.*, 217. The inference is crystal clear—if the Indians turned themselves over to the Fort Lyon military they would be safe from attack by soldiers.

[14] *Ibid.*, 91.

first with Wynkoop, Soule, John Smith, and others, then to another shot by themselves, producing the only known photographs of Black Kettle.

Wynkoop remained in Denver for a few days, during which time he offered reassurances to farmers from along the Arkansas Valley that they could return to their ranches in perfect safety.

When Wynkoop arrived back at Fort Lyon with the Cheyenne and Arapaho chiefs, he held another council, telling them they could go out and bring in their villages to a place near the post where he could prevent any difficulties with other whites. The chiefs were willing to do whatever Wynkoop requested of them, expressing full confidence in him. Wynkoop also asked Black Kettle to bring in the other three captives as soon as possible. The Cheyenne principal chief promised to do this, but said that it would be difficult and take some time, as those prisoners were off at a distance with some of Bull Bear's band.[15] The chiefs then left to join their tribes, and on October 8, Wynkoop dispatched Lieutenant Denison to General Curtis at Leavenworth with a full report on his dealings with the Indians. He concluded:

> I think that if some terms are made with these Indians, I can arrange matters so, by bringing their villages under my direct control, that I can answer for their fidelity. We are at war with the Sioux, and the Kiowas, and Comanches; these Indians, the Arapahoes and Cheyennes, tell me they are willing to lend me their assistance in fighting the Kiowas and Comanches. . . . I know that in a general Indian war it will take more soldiers than we can possibly spare to keep open the two lines of communication, protect the settlements, and make an effective war upon them.[16]

15 *Ibid.*, 91–92.   16 *Ibid.*, 121.

About ten days later some 113 lodges of Arapahoes (652 Indians by count) under Left Hand and Little Raven came in to Lyon and camped two miles from the post. Since they were in destitute condition, Wynkoop issued them prisoner allowance for ten days. The Arapahoes were given the run of the post, and many came in to trade buffalo skins for provisions of any kind.[17] During this time, the chiefs appeared at the headquarters one day and reported that a large party of Utes were in the vicinity. They requested the protection of the soldiers. Wynkoop mounted twenty men and with Soule rode out to the Arapaho camp, but found that the report was a false alarm.[18]

On November 5, Major Scott J. Anthony arrived at Fort Lyon from Kansas, carrying orders from General Curtis to relieve Wynkoop as commander of the post. Wynkoop was ordered to report to District Headquarters at Fort Riley, Kansas. There had been complaints that the Indians were running things at Fort Lyon. Anthony carried strict orders not to have anything to do with the Indians, to make them no issues, and to keep them away from the post.[19] On the sixth, Anthony reported from Lyon:

[17] *Ibid.*, 61; *Rebellion Records,* Series I, Vol. XLI, Part I, 912.

[18] "Sand Creek Massacre," 101, 117.

[19] *Rebellion Records,* Series I, Vol. XLI, Part IV, 62.

There is no evidence to support the claim that Chivington instigated this move in order to get rid of Wynkoop at Fort Lyon. Clearly the order was Curtis' responsibility, though Major Henning at Fort Riley District Headquarters (now covering Fort Lyon) issued it. Henning wrote Anthony: "I am very desirous to have an officer of judgment at Fort Lyon, and especially one that will not committ any such foolish acts as are reported to have occurred there." The order stated in part: ". . . investigate and report upon the unofficial rumors that reach headquarters that certain officers have issued stores, goods, or supplies to hostile Indians. . . ." *Ibid.* Who brought the rumors to Fort Riley is anybody's guess.

Nine Cheyenne Indians to-day sent in, wishing to see me. They state that 600 of that tribe are now 35 miles north of here, coming towards the post, and 2,000 about 75 miles away, waiting for better weather to enable them to come in. I shall not permit them to come in, even as prisoners, for the reason that if I do, I shall have to subsist them upon a prisoner's rations. I shall, however, demand their arms, all stolen stock, and the perpetrators of all depredations. I am of the opinion that they will not accept this proposition, but that they will return to the Smoky Hill. They pretend that they want peace, and I think they do now, as they cannot fight during the winter, except where a small band of them can find an unprotected train or frontier settlement. I do not think it is policy to make peace with them now, until all perpetrators of depredations are surrendered up to be dealt with as we may propose.[20]

When Wynkoop and the others explained the recent history of the situation to Anthony and outlined Wynkoop's policy, however, Anthony acknowledged that he would be forced to follow the same course of action. He issued rations to the Arapahoes, but at the same time he directed them to give up their arms and all horses and mules which belonged to the government or to white citizens. The Indians complied with this, giving up three rifles, one pistol, about sixty bows and quivers, four horses, and ten mules.[21]

[20] "Massacre of Cheyenne Indians," 70–71; Rebellion Records, Series I, Vol. XLI, Part I, 913–14.

[21] Ibid.

William H. Valentine, a soldier of the First Cavalry, stated that the Indians, Arapahoes under Little Raven and Left Hand who were in camp across the river from Fort Lyon, had eight head of mules which had been taken during the Snyder murders near Booneville. The mules were annoying the post herd, but Wynkoop had issued orders not to meddle with them until the Indian difficulty was settled. "Sand Creek Massacre," 225–26.

Wynkoop was visiting the Arapaho camp when Anthony came up, secreted a company of cavalry to watch the encampment, and entered to talk with the

In the meantime, One-Eye had arrived at the Caddoe ranch of his son-in-law, John Prowers,[22] and gone into camp there. A few days later Black Kettle, whose village was then in camp at Sand Creek, and a party of some sixty or seventy Cheyenne men appeared at Fort Lyon. A consultation with the Indians was called by Anthony, with John Smith and Prowers interpreting.[23]

The Cheyennes said that the Arapahoes had reported that things "looked dark" since the "red-eye chief"[24] had arrived at Fort Lyon and wanted to know what the situation was.

Indians, ordering them to give up the United States and citizens' stock and collecting their arms. Anthony reported: "Their arms are in very poor condition and but few, with little ammunition. Their horses are far below the average grade of Indians' horses. In fact, these that are here could make but a feeble fight if they desired war. . . ." *Rebellion Records*, Series I, Vol. XLI, Part I, 913–14.

But Anthony ordered his guards to fire at the Indians who came to the post, and the soldier Valentine stated: "Some few hours afterwards he [Anthony] was laughing at the idea of seeing the Indians run. He said that they had annoyed him enough, and that was the only way to get rid of them, or words to that effect." "Sand Creek Massacre," 226.

Simeon Whiteley, in a letter to Senator Doolittle, wrote that Anthony said to him: ". . . two days before Colonel Chivington came down the Cheyennes sent word to me, after I had fired on them, if he would go up to their camp they would give him all he wanted . . . I told Colonel Chivington I was glad he had come, that I would have gone before and cleaned out the sons of guns if I had had force enough; but there were some of them I should have saved if possible." "The Chivington Massacre," 91.

[22] John Prowers came to Bent's Fort in 1856 with Agent Robert C. Miller and, induced by good wages and situation, remained in Bent's employ as a clerk. In 1861 he married fifteen-year-old Amache Ochinee, daughter of Cheyenne subchief One-Eye and, like Bent, was respected by the Cheyenne as a friend and advisor. In 1863 he purchased some land from Bent across the river from the new fort and entered into the ranching business, herding government cattle, horses, and mules.

[23] "Sand Creek Massacre," 46, 87, 104–106; "Massacre of Cheyenne Indians," 31.

[24] Anthony was "red-eyed" from scurvy, contacted at Lyon in 1863.

Receiving permission from Anthony to say a few words, Wynkoop told the Indians that it was true that he was no longer in command, having been replaced by Anthony, who was a good chief and would treat them as he had treated them. Anthony then spoke, telling the chiefs that he had heard a great many bad reports about them before he came to Lyon and had expected to have a fight with them. But since his arrival, he said, he had found things quite different than he had expected and he would do everything he could to make a lasting peace. At present he could not issue rations to them, but he hoped that the next mail would bring news that he could give them something to eat. He suggested that in the meantime the Indians remain on Sand Creek where their men could hunt buffalo. He agreed that when he received news he would let them know about it, good or bad, in line with Major Wynkoop's promise.[25]

Black Kettle replied that he was perfectly satisfied with what he had heard. He had intended to move on to the Purgatoire with his tribe, but would remain at Sand Creek as Anthony suggested. He also hoped they would hear from the States soon as his people could not stay long without food. When he stated that it was his intention to go on down the river the next day and visit Colonel Bent, Anthony replied that he had nothing at the fort to give the Indians to eat nor any place to keep them for the night.

John Prowers then asked permission to take them to his place. Prowers fed the Cheyenne group that night, and the next morning Black Kettle and a part of his band left for Bent's, returning the following day. Black Kettle told Prowers that he was sorry that the "tall chief" was leaving, but that the

25 "Massacre of Cheyenne Indians," 17–18.

Indians were satisfied with the way things were going and hoped the matter would soon be settled. The next morning Prowers gave the Indians a few presents—sugar, coffee, flour, rice, and bacon, plus some tobacco which the officers of the post had bought for them. Anthony had promised to ride down and have another talk with Black Kettle, but instead he sent John Smith to reassure the Cheyennes that they would be perfectly safe at Sand Creek. They returned to their village at the Smoky Hill crossing of Sand Creek, while Little Raven moved his Arapahoes down the Arkansas near the mouth of Sand Creek. Left Hand, ill, took eight of his lodges to Sand Creek with Black Kettle.[26]

Anthony's attitude toward the Indians is a matter of clear record in his report made to Curtis on November 16 from Fort Lyon:

> I told them that I was not authorized as yet to say that any permanent peace could be established, but that *no war would be waged against them until your pleasure was heard.* I am satisfied that all of the Arapahoes and Cheyennes who have visited this post desire peace, yet many of their men of these bands are now on the Smoky Hill and Platte, having in their possession a large amount of stock. I have been trying to let the Indians that I have talked with think that I have no desire for trouble with them, but that I could not agree upon a permanent peace until I was authorized by you, thus keeping matters quiet for the present, and until troops enough are sent out to enforce any demand we may choose to make. It would be easy for us to fight the few Indian warriors that have come into the post, but as soon as we assume a hostile attitude the travel upon the road will be cut off, and the settlements above

[26] *Ibid.*, 31. Anthony employed One-Eye as a spy to report on hostile movements in the region.

and upon the different streams will be completely broken up, as we are not strong enough to follow them and fight them upon their own ground. Some of the Cheyenne and Arapahoe Indians can be made useful to us. . . . My intention, however, is to let matters remain dormant until troops can be sent out to take the field against all the tribes.[27]

On November 26, Wynkoop left Fort Lyon for Kansas by stage with an escort of cavalry. With him he carried two letters testifying to the support of his policy with the Indians. One, written by Lieutenant Cramer and "bearing testimony to the fact that the course adopted and carried out by you was the only proper one to pursue,"[28] was signed by all the officers at Fort Lyon and endorsed with a note of approval by Anthony. The other, signed by twenty-seven citizens who lived in the Arkansas Valley, stated that the signers "desire to express to you our hearty sympathy in your laudable efforts to prevent further danger and bloodshed, and sincerely congratulate you in your noble efforts to do what we consider right, politic, and just."[29]

Wynkoop reported that two days after leaving Lyon he was

[27] *Rebellion Records*, Series I, Vol. XLI, Part I, 914.

[28] "Sand Creek Massacre," 93–94.

[29] *Ibid.*, 95.

General Curtis was much in the dark concerning the Indian problem. With Price chased back into Arkansas, Curtis turned to the matter of the Indians about whom Major Henning at Fort Riley and others were pressing him. On December 2, 1864 (after the Sand Creek Massacre, but before Curtis learned of it), he wrote Henning: "The treaty operations at Lyon greatly embarrass matters, and I hope you have disposed of Major Wynkoop and directed a change for the better. . . . I am going to send troops forward with a view of further operations at the proper time. . . . Of course, I have my eyes on the matter of Indian troubles." *Rebellion Records,* Series I, Vol. XLI, Part IV, 751.

On December 5 he wrote to Governor Evans in Washington: "I confess myself entirely undecided and uncertain as to what can be done with such nominal Indian prisoners." *Ibid.,* 771–72.

overtaken by three Indians who were led by the Arapaho No-ta-nee. They had been sent by Black Kettle to warn Wynkoop that some two hundred Sioux had left the headwaters of the Smoky Hill for the purpose of making war along the Arkansas. Wynkoop proceeded cautiously to Larned, and while there he learned that a body of Sioux had been seen along the river.[30]

On the same day that Wynkoop left Lyon, John Smith, a soldier, and a teamster in the employ of Dexter Colley, left the post for the Cheyenne village at Sand Creek with a load of trade goods.

[30] "Sand Creek Massacre," 87. Wynkoop's stage was met at Fort Larned by the westbound stage carrying Julia Lambert, who was returning to Fort Lyon from Fort Leavenworth.

VIII.

THE
BLOODLESS
THIRD

When governor evans received authority on August 11 to raise a mounted regiment of hundred-day volunteers, recruiting commissions were sent out immediately. Posters were put up, war meetings held, speeches made, and men began to muster into the Third Regiment of the Colorado Volunteer Cavalry. In order to promote enlistments, the businessmen of Denver had petitioned Colonel Chivington to establish martial law, and on August 23 he issued a proclamation to that effect.[1] Houses of trade, except the dispensaries of medicine for the sick, were forbidden to open, and grocery and other provisions stores were allowed to open only three hours each day. All trains and wagons were forbidden to leave the territory. It was hoped by these measures to complete the enlist-

[1] *Rocky Mountain News*, Denver, August 23, 1864, p. 3.

ments in the Third Regiment.[2] At the same time business entrepreneurs began scrambling for contracts in equipping the new outfit.

Almost as soon as each company unit was formed and men had drawn ordnance and clothing stores—there was a limited supply—the troops were placed on garrison duty along the Platte route. A company of hundred-day men was dispatched in late August to Fort Lupton, one to Valley Station, one to Junction and another to Latham.[3] Other companies were in training at newly established Camp Evans a couple of miles above Denver. Mounts for the units were purchased at random from among the Colorado populace, everything from ponies to plow horses. The guns issued were largely out-of-date Austrian muzzle-loading muskets of large bore.[4]

A good deal of rivalry had existed for the position of commanding officer of the Third, and several of Denver's prominent citizens were recommended for the job, either by someone else or by themselves. Chivington, however, had become thoroughly impressed with Lieutenant George L. Shoup, who deserved much of the credit for the capture of the Reynolds gang and who was a member of the State Constitutional Convention held in July, and when asked for an opinion by Evans, Chivington unhesitantly penned a recommendation for him. On September 21, Evans appointed Shoup as commanding colonel of the Third Colorado Cavalry.[5]

[2] "Nathaniel P. Hill Inspects Colorado, Letters Written in 1864," *The Colorado Magazine*, Vol. XXXIV (1957), 33, footnote 11.

[3] *Rebellion Records*, Series I, Vol. XLI, Part II, 946.

[4] Irving Howbert, *Memories of a Lifetime in the Pike's Peak Region*, 119.

[5] "Sand Creek Massacre," 175.

Leavitt L. Bowen was appointed Lieutenant Colonel; W. F. Wilder, First Major; Hal Sayr, Second Major; and Samuel Logan, Third Major. Company

Along the Platte, things were relatively quiet. A party of ten Cheyennes, reportedly coming from the north, raided Gerry's ranch and stole 150 head of cattle on August 21.[6] But at Fort Lupton, Captain S. E. Browne's scouting parties were finding only few signs of Indians, and his recruits were growing restless and wanting to transfer to another area where there would be more action.[7]

Also on the twenty-first a group of Indians attacked a horse herd belonging to a detachment of Colorado First at Jimmy's Camp near Colorado City. The Indians made off with the herd.[8] Again on the same day, three men were attacked by what was at first believed to be Indians near Russellville, south of Denver. Two escaped and one was missing. Taking a party of thirty men, Colorado Ranger Captain A. J. Gill went to the scene of the battle, finding the man's hat full of arrow holes and his rifle broken. The smashed gun and the fact that a brass clock—the Indians were fond of brass—had been broken and left behind made Gill think that the attackers might have been guerrillas.[9]

On September 4, Colley wrote of One-Eye's arrival at Fort Lyon, reporting to Governor Evans that the Cheyennes and

Commanding Officers of the Third were: Company A, Lieutenant Theodore Cree; Company B, Captain H. M. Orahood; Company C, Captain William Morgan; Company D, Captain David Nichols; Company E, Captain Jay J. Johnson; Company F, Captain Ed Chase; Company G, Captain Oliver H. P. Baxter; Company H, Captain Henry D. Williams; Company I, Captain John McCannon; Company K, Captain Adam L. Shock; Company L, Captain J. Freeman Phillips; Company M, Captain Presley Talbot. *Rocky Mountain News*, October 7, 1864, p. 1.

[6] *Rebellion Records*, Series I, Vol. XLI, Part II, 843.

[7] *Ibid.*, 810.

[8] *Ibid.*

[9] *Ibid.*, 844.

Ogallala and Brule Sioux were gathered at the Bunch of Timbers.[10] Evans passed the information on to Chivington.

Chivington, in the meantime, was trying to get the Third outfitted and equipped, taking the shortcuts on which he prided himself, and on September 19 he wired Stanton that a train with ordnance stores was delayed at Fort Lyon and requested authority to divert the stores, which were headed for General Carleton's New Mexico command, for the Colorado Third. He indicated that he planned to use the supplies against the "Indian warriors congregated eighty miles from Lyon, three thousand strong."[11] Major General Halleck, army chief of staff, replied that Chivington must make requisition for his wants in the usual way.[12] Chivington tried again, this time wiring Halleck, "Have regiment of 100 days men ready for field. Train on the way from Fort Leavenworth, but cannot get here in time because of the Indian troubles on the Platte route. Are four hundred miles back, and laid up. The time of this regiment will expire and Indians will still hold road. This is no ordinary case."[13]

Halleck again replied, pointedly telling Chivington to communicate his wants to his superior officer, General Curtis.[14]

Though Indian depredations had definitely increased in Colorado Territory, the war of extermination, which Evans had been writing to Washington about, had failed to materialize. Shortly after the council with the Indian chiefs in Denver, Evans left for council with the Utes. Curtis wired Chivington of Blunt's fight on the Pawnee Fork, stating that the Indians

10 *Rebellion Records*, Series I, Vol. XLI, Part III, 195.
11 "Massacre of Cheyenne Indians," 68.
12 *Ibid.*
13 *Ibid.*
14 *Ibid.*

were probably the same ones with whom Wynkoop had been dealing and that they were headed for the Smoky Hill.[15] Chivington promised that he would keep his eye out for them.

On October 10, Captain Nichols of the Colorado Third, in camp at Valley Station on the Platte, learned of the presence of a small band of Indians, took out forty troops, and found two lodges camped at a spring in the bluffs south of the river. Nichols commenced battle, killed six warriors, three women, and one boy about fourteen years of age, and captured ten ponies and a mule. In one of the lodges the soldiers found a white woman's scalp and articles of clothing, plus bills of lading from St. Joseph to Denver. The Indians were Cheyennes and were led by Big Wolf. "We also found Big Wolf's certificates of good character, friendship for whites, &c., but the lady's scalp and clothing failed to corroborate the statements."[16]

This was the first blood for the Colorado Third, but in Denver some had already dubbed the new regiment the "Bloodless Third," for it had begun to appear as though most of the hundred-day men were going to reach the end of their enlistment without having engaged in battle.[17] The men were beginning to complain strongly that their understanding upon enlistment was that they were to be given active service against the Indians.[18]

It had become increasingly apparent that most of the Indians were gone from the South Platte, and Chivington began moving his Colorado Third units to Bijou Basin, located in a

[15] *Rebellion Records,* Series I, Vol. XLI, Part III, 696.
[16] *Ibid.,* 789–99.
[17] Lynn I. Perrigo, "Major Hal Sayre's Diary of the Sand Creek Campaign," *The Colorado Magazine,* Vol. XV (1928), footnote 46.
[18] Howbert, *Memories of a Lifetime,* 120.

circular valley at the juncture of several streams sixty miles southeast of Denver. On October 16 he wrote to Wynkoop at Lyon, requesting that he speed up the shipment of some Starr carbines which he said he intended to use in going after a large number of Indians on the Republican.[19]

Late in October, Chivington received a telegram that made his plans for an Indian campaign even more urgent. The wire was from Brigadier-General P. E. Connor at Salt Lake City. Connor, commanding the Department af Utah, had received instructions from Stanton to give all protection in his power to the overland stage between Salt Lake City and Fort Kearny. Connor planned to take two companies of his cavalry out, and wired Chivington to ask "Can we get a fight out of Indians this winter? Can you send grain out on road to meet my command? How many troops can you spare for a campaign? Answer."[20]

Chivington was alarmed to the extreme, wiring Curtis, "Have department lines been changed? If not, will I allow him to give direction to matters within this district? Line perfectly protected to Julesburg. The line this side of Julesburg ought to be in this district, as my troops are taking care of it."[21]

The Territory of Colorado, meanwhile had been involved in a heated controversy over statehood. Governor Evans, who had been running for a United States Senate seat should the bill be passed, withdrew from the race because it was felt he was hurting the statehood movement. The statehood issue was defeated, nevertheless, in the election held in early November.

[19] *Rebellion Records,* Series I, Vol. XLI, Part IV, 23–24.
[20] *Ibid.,* 259.
[21] *Ibid.*

Chivington was badly beaten by Allen A. Bradford, 4,625 to 2,830 votes, for the position of delegate to Congress for two years representing the Territory of Colorado. But Chivington's popularity was proved when he ran for Congress as a specialty on the statehood ticket. Here he defeated Bradford 3,652 votes to 479, a futile victory with statehood defeated.[22]

On November 14, Connor, accompanied by Ben Holliday, arrived in Denver to inspect the matter of protecting the stage line, and on the very same day Chivington issued marching orders to the Colorado Third.[23] An account written by Chivington himself offers much insight into the matter:

> Several days before the troops left Denver General Conor [sic], who was in command of the district of Utah, had been in Denver, and my impression from the day of his coming was that he had been ordered here by the secretary of war, to see whether we were efficiently prosecuting this campaign against the Indians.
>
> In this conviction I was confirmed when the general came to me, after I had mounted to overtake the troops, and said to me:
>
> "I think from the temper of the men that you have and all I can learn that you will give these Indians a most terrible threshing if you catch them, and if it was in the mountains, and you had them in a canon, and your troops at one end of it and the Bear river at the other, as I had the Pi-Utes, you could catch them; but I am afraid on these plains you won't do it."
>
> I said: "Possibly I may not, but I think I shall."
>
> "Well," he said, "I repeat, if you catch them—but I don't think you will—you will give them a good dressing down."

[22] *Rocky Mountain News*, November 4, 1864, p. 2.

[23] Connor was received by Evans and Chivington and entertained with a serenade by the Colorado First's band. Evans left for Washington November 16. *Ibid.*, November 16, 1864.

To which I could only reply: "I may not, general, but I think I will catch them." And as I was about to ride off he said:

"If you do catch them wire me just as soon as you can get to a telegraph office, for I shall want to know it, and I start by the next coach for Salt Lake."

I promised him I would do so, when he looked back at me and said:

"Colonel, where are these Indians?"

I said: "General, that is the trick that wins in this game, if the game is won. There are but two persons who know their exact location, and they are myself and Colonel George L. Shoup."[24]

Chivington headed the Colorado Third, plus three companies of the Colorado First, toward the Arkansas. Seven companies which had been assembled at Bijou Basin moved out in deeply-drifted snow toward Camp Fillmore under Major Sayr, while Colonel Shoup went up the Platte to pick up the companies of the Third at Junction and Valley Station.[25]

The weather was extremely cold, and often horse and rider would go nearly out of sight in the snow-drifted gulches. Sayr arrived at Fillmore on November 18, finding Company E of the Colorado First already in camp there. Three days later Shoup arrived with companies C, D, and F of the Third and

[24] *The Denver Republican,* May 18, 1890.

Connor, too, knew where the Indians were, as he proved in a letter to Halleck on November 21, 1864. Chivington had refused him use of Colorado troops for an expedition against the Indians "who, I am credibly informed, are now in winter quarters on the Republican Fork and the Arkansas River." He further stated, and correctly, "Any expedition against the Indians which would not probably result in their signal chastisement, would be productive of harm rather than good, and until suitable arrangements to that end shall have been made, I do not deem it wise or prudent either to undertake or advise a campaign against them." *Rebellion Records,* Series I, Vol. XLI, Part 1, 908–10.

[25] Perrigo, *The Colorado Magazine,* Vol. XV (1928), 41–57.

Company H of the First. He had brought old Jim Beckwith from Denver along as a guide. On the twenty-third, Sayr noted in his diary, "Wednesday Nov. 23d/64. Col. Chivington—Maj Downing & Capt Jo Maynard A.A.A.G. arrived from Denver this evening—Regiment inspected this evening about dark—Chivington takes command which gives pretty general dissatisfaction—"[26]

Early the next day Chivington's command broke camp and began their march eastward along the Arkansas, covering fifteen miles on November 24 and twelve miles the next day to reach Spring Bottom, a stage station along the Arkansas. Here was a good camping place, wood and water in abundance, and a cabin where Chivington and his officers could warm their bottoms and fill their bellies.

That evening James Combs from Lyon entered the station. He and another man were on their way to Pueblo, and Chivington began questioning him concerning the status of things at Fort Lyon. Upon learning of Wynkoop's leaving for Fort Larned, Chivington surmised laughingly that Wynkoop must have been placed in charge of "that post." When Combs made reference to Wynkoop's being in charge before Anthony, Chivington jokingly corrected him by saying that it was Left Hand who had *really* been in charge of Lyon. While Combs ate his supper, the officers talked about the scalps they would take and how they were going to arrange them.[27]

[26] *Ibid.*
[27] "Sand Creek Massacre," 115.

Combs testified that when he finished his meal and rose to leave, Chivington drew himself up in his chair and remarked: "Well, I long to be wading in gore." *Ibid.*, 117.

Cross-examination by Chivington implied that such "remarks of hatred as uttered by Chivington" were in reply to what Combs had said in regard to the Indians. *Ibid.*, 118.

The weather had turned off comfortably warm, and the next morning the command made good time, twenty-eight miles, to camp a half mile above Bent's Old Fort, now serving as a junction of the Santa Fe and Denver coach lines. On the twenty-seventh, Sunday they marched 38 miles and camped 14 miles above Fort Lyon. Lieutenant Graham with a squad of Colorado Third men was ordered to cross the river to Bent's ranch at the mouth of the Purgatoire and put the place under guard, allowing no one to leave.[28] Shortly down-river, Captain Cook of the First was dispatched with similar orders to the ranch house of John Prowers at the mouth of the Caddoe.[29]

On the evening of November 27, Si Soule[30] and Second

[28] *Ibid.*, 51.

[29] *Ibid.*, 107.

[30] Silas S. Soule had come west to Kansas Territory in 1854 with his father, Amasa Soule, who helped to establish the first underground railroad station for escaping slaves. Silas assisted in his father's activities, cutting his teeth as one of the original Kansas jayhawkers. The Soule family was of English descent, but as a boy Si had worked in a factory where most of the employees were Irish and while there developed a knack for talking with an Irish brogue. This, combined with a jolly and playful nature, caused many people to think him Irish. In 1859 he played a leading role in the then famous Doy rescue party.

As a result of the notoriety received from this affair, Soule and two others of the rescue party were selected to assist in a daring plan to rescue John Brown from his cell at Harper's Ferry. This rescue was never attempted, largely because such a feat was virtually impossible and because John Brown himself refused to be rescued, prefering to become a martyr to his cause. A similar effort was made to save two of the men captured with Brown, and again Soule played a leading role:

"During the middle of February a secret message was received by the prisoners and a reply returned. An intoxicated man was arrested in Charlestown on a Saturday evening and locked up over Sunday in jail. To all appearances he was a jolly, devil-may-care young Irish laborer (Silas S. Soule), in whom whiskey left nothing but boisterous fun. As he sobered up he became a delight to the jailer's family by his funny songs and witty words. Discipline

Lieutenant Minton, the latter of the First New Mexico Volunteers, spotted campfires while riding west of Fort Lyon. Returning to the post, they reported the matter to Anthony, speculating that the fires must belong to Indians, "Kiowas" perhaps, since Cheyennes or Arapahoes would have likely come on in to the fort. There had been a noticeable absence of travel and mail from the direction of Denver during the past three weeks, and it had been suggested that Indian trouble was to blame.[31] Anthony ordered Soule to investigate, and before sunup on the twenty-eighth he led a company of twenty troops of Colorado First on a scout up the Arkansas.[32]

Ten miles above the fort, Soule's command came upon a mule team and wagon headed down the north bank of the river toward Lyon. Soule inquired if the driver had seen Indians on the trail behind. The man replied he had not, but that Colonel Chivington from Denver was back there with ten or twelve companies of one hundred "daysers."

had relaxed, vigilance nodded, and the careless Irishman was enabled to communicate with Stevens and Hazlett." O. E. Morse, "An Attempted Rescue of John Brown From Charlestown, Va., Jail," *Kansas State Historical Society*, Vol. VIII, 213–26.

But again the prisoners refused to be saved, and they were hanged on schedule. Soule returned to Kansas, via Philadelphia, where he met and became friends with some of the Eastern abolitionists, including the noted poet, Walt Whitman. Once back in Kansas, Soule found the gold rush in full swing, and he too headed for the mountains where he helped make the gulch now known as Geneva. When the war broke out Soule recruited for the First Regiment of Colorado Volunteers and took a commission as lieutenant. He was with the Volunteers when they defeated the Texans at the Battle of La Glorieta Pass in the spring of 1862. Ovando J. Hollister wrote: "Robbins, Soule and Hardin were here, every one of them as cool and collected as if on parade." Hollister, *Boldly They Rode, A History of the First Colorado Regiment of Volunteers*, 70.

[31] "The Chivington Massacre," 27–28.

[32] "Sand Creek Massacre," 10.

This was surprising information. There had been no advance notice that Chivington was on his way, nor, as far as anyone at Lyon knew, any reason for his appearing with such a force. Quickly Soule moved on and within two miles, at the mouth of Rule Creek, came up to the advance of a long, four-abreast column of blue-overcoated cavalry. At their lead was the massive figure of John Chivington, who inquired of Soule if they knew he was coming at Fort Lyon. Soule answered in the negative, that he had only learned the fact a few minutes before from the driver of the mule team. Chivington then asked if there were any Indians at the fort. Soule replied that there were some Cheyennes and Arapahoes camped not far from the post. He stressed that they were not dangerous, were considered as prisoners, and were waiting to hear from General Curtis. According to Soule, one of the officers with Chivington said, "They won't be prisoners after we get there," and drew a laugh from the others.

Chivington, concerned that the mule team should reach Lyon before his command, rode ahead of the column toward the fort, accompanied by Major Downing. The command reached Lyon around noon and went into camp below the commissary. Chivington immediately threw a cordon of pickets around the post with orders that no one would be allowed to leave, under penalty of death.[33]

Anthony met Chivington and Downing by the officers' quarters and welcomed them heartily and approvingly, now saying openly what he had been writing in his reports—that he felt the Indians should be punished and would have attacked them long ago had he had the force. He was all for the

[33] *Ibid.*, 11, 165.

expedition and was eager to join it with his Fort Lyon troops, every man of which he claimed would go.[34]

Preparation for the campaign began at once. Forage—hay and corn—was issued for Chivington's stock, and the men each drew rations of bacon and hardtack which they packed in their saddle bags. Chivington, determined that the element of surprise should not be taken from him, issued marching orders for eight o'clock that same evening.

When Soule arrived back at the post, he had immediately sought out Lieutenants Cramer and Baldwin and discussed the plan to attack the Indians at Sand Creek. They were in full agreement that Chivington should be dissuaded, and Soule went to his commanding officer, Anthony, about the matter, expecting his support. Instead, he found that Anthony, who had promised to carry out Wynkoop's policies with the Indians, was now singing an entirely different tune. Soule stated:

> I talked to Anthony about it, and he said that some of those Indians ought to be killed; that he had been only waiting for a good chance to pitch into them. I reminded him of the pledges he had made them, and he said that Colonel Chivington had told him that those Indians he had pledged the soldiers and the white men in the camp should not be killed; that the object of the expedition was to go out to the Smoky Hill and follow the Indians up. Anthony told me that I would not compromise myself by going out, as I was opposed to going.[35]

Soule was further warned by Anthony, Cramer, and others

[34] *Ibid.*, 179, 182, 208, 212; "Massacre of Cheyenne Indians," 108; "The Chivington Massacre," 69–70.
[35] "Sand Creek Massacre," 25.

THE SAND CREEK MASSACRE

not to go to the camp where Chivington was, that Chivington had made threats against Soule for his opposition to the plan. Cramer also tried to reason with Anthony, stating that he thought Black Kettle and his tribe had acted in good faith, that they had saved the lives of the hundred and twenty soldiers at the Smoky Hill as well as the settlers in the Arkansas Valley. Anthony promised Cramer that Black Kettle and his friends would be spared and that the object of the expedition was to surround the camp and take stolen stock and kill only those Indians that had been committing depredations.[36]

Cramer also had his try with Chivington:

I had some conversation with Major Downing, Lieutenant Maynard, and Colonel Chivington. I stated to them my feelings in regards to the matter; that I believed it to be "murder," and stated the obligations that we of Major Wynkoop's command were under to those Indians. To Colonel Chivington I know I stated that Major Wynkoop had pledged his word as an officer and a man to those Indians, and that all officers under him were indirectly pledged in the same manner that he was, and that I felt it was placing us in very embarrassing circumstances to fight the same Indians that had saved our lives, as we all felt they had. Colonel Chivington's reply was, that he believed it to be right or honorable to use any means under God's heaven to kill Indians that would kill women and chil-

36 *Ibid.,* 46–47.

Reporting to headquarters at Fort Riley concerning Chivington's arrival and plans, Anthony said: "I have the honor to report that Col. John M. Chivington, First Cavalry of Colorado, arrived at this post this day with 1,000 men of the Third Colorado Cavalry (100-days' men) and two howitzers, on expedition against Indians. This number of men has been required for some time, and is appreciated by me now, as I believe the Indians will be properly punished—what they have for some time deserved. I go out with 125 men and two howitzers to join his command." *Rebellion Records,* Series I, Vol. XLI, Part IV, 708. This, in Anthony's own words, is disproof that he argued against the expedition.

142

dren, and "damn any man that was in sympathy with Indians," and such men as Major Wynkoop and myself had better get out of the United States service.[37]

A final attempt to divert the huge former preacher was made that night in the office of Lieutenant Cossitt. Present were Cossitt, Lieutenant Minton, Major Colley, Lieutenant Maynard, Captain Cook, Chivington, and a few Fort Lyon civilians.

Minton and Cossitt upheld Wynkoop's course of action and stated their opinion that it would be a crime to attack Indians who were considered to be prisoners. Colley, too, upheld Wynkoop, claiming that the Cheyennes had been misunderstood, misrepresented, and ill-treated by Parmetar and others. Chivington, livid with anger at this mounting opposition, walked excitedly around the room and ended the meeting by once more declaring "Damn any man who is in sympathy with an Indian!"[38]

At eight o'clock that night, the twenty-eighth, campfires were snuffed and the command fell into formation with three days' cooked rations and twenty uncooked. There were between 675 and 700 troops in all: some 450 Colorado Third men under Colonel Shoup, 100 to 125 Colorado First under Lieutenant Wilson, and 125 Fort Lyon Colorado First troops under Anthony. These were divided into five battalions under Lieutenant Colonel Bowen, Major Sayr, Captain Cree, Lieutenant Wilson, and Major Anthony. On Chivington's field staff were Major Downing and A. J. Gill, captain of territorial militia, who served as a volunteer aid. The small army boasted four pieces of artillery, twelve-pound mountain howitzers,

[37] "Sand Creek Massacre," 47.
[38] *Ibid.*, 147, 153, 156; "The Chivington Massacre," 34, 54, 62.

two of which were assigned to Bowen's Company C of the Colorado Third and two were under the command of Lieutenant Baldwin and Company G of the First. Soule commanded Company D, Colorado First, and Cramer, Company K. Captain Cook was left in charge of the post. Robert Bent had been pressed into service as guide to help Jim Beckwith.[39]

Among those who watched Chivington's army disappear over the bluffs into the night was Lieutenant Colonel Samuel Tappan. He had returned from visiting General Grant at City Point only two days before and had injured his foot while riding a horse at Fort Lyon.

[39] Julia S. Lambert states that Chivington attached Robert Bent, who had previously served as a guide and interpreter for Anthony, to his force when passing his ranch near Spring Bottom. "Plain Tales of the Plains," *The Trail*, Vol. VIII (1916), No. 12, 11.

```
╔══════════════════════════════╗
║                              ║
║            IX.               ║
║                              ║
║          MASSACRE            ║
║             AT               ║
║         SAND CREEK           ║
║                              ║
║                              ║
╚══════════════════════════════╝
```

THE COMMAND TRAVELED in columns of fours, rapidly in cavalry walk-trot-gallop-dismount and lead style. It was a clear
and bright starlit night, and the air which at first seemed
merely crisp soon became uncomfortably cool. Around midnight the troops found themselves being led through one of
the shallow lakes that spotted the plains above Lyon, and
someone suspected that the half-blood Robert Bent was
attempting to get their ammunition wet so that their paper
cartridges would crack and spoil. Some of them grew sleepy
and nibbled on the hardtack rations to keep awake, only to
discover later that it was "very much alive" with bugs.[1]

The march continued throughout the night without inter-
mission, until finally the first light of November 29, 1864, rose

[1] Irving Howbert, *Memories of a Lifetime in the Pike's Peak Region,* 122.

up from the flat horizon to the east and spread over the sand hills. To their right, the troops could see the tree-marked course of a river. The Big Sandy, someone said.

Shortly after the sun had appeared, Chivington and Shoup, riding in advance of the troops, reached the crest of a rise and saw that the creek curved leftward sharply across their line of march.[2] It was here that a range of sand bluffs blocked the southerly flow of Sand Creek, causing it to make a graceful bend to a nearly east-west course for a mile or so before arcing in a wide loop back to the south again. Beyond the bluffs the land fell away, swelling up again in the far distance.

The river had no prominent north bank, the sand hills to the south having caught the main force of past flood waters, and the inside arc of the river bed, worn more gradually, was low and flat. Only a faint trickle of water snaked its way along the creek bed, and this was ice-crusted. In the bend grew a scattering of cottonwood and willow, and through the bare tops a horse herd could be seen grazing. To the west, less than a mile away, the village of Black Kettle's Cheyennes speckled the river's bend on the north bank. The lodges, quickly esti-mated at more than a hundred, gleamed in the early light. The yapping of camp dogs and hurried movements among the lodges indicated that the soldiers had been spotted.

Chivington moved quickly, dispatching Lieutenant Wil-son with Companies C, E, and F of the First in a charge across the creek to cut between the herd and the village. Captain McCannon and Company I of the Third were directed by

[2] This account of the Sand Creek affair is based upon numerous testi-monies, official reports, and affidavits regarding the incident to be found in the following sources "Sand Creek Massacre"; "The Chivington Massacre"; "Massacre of Cheyenne Indians"; and *Rebellion Records*. Only specific items will be footnoted in the remainder of this chapter.

146

BLACK KETTLE AND CHIEFS IN DENVER—SEPTEMBER, 1864
At center, holding the peace pipe, is Black Kettle. White Antelope is on his far right, Neva is between them, and Bull Bear is on Black Kettle's left. Wynkoop and Soule are in front, while third from the left in the back is John Smith.

Courtesy Library, State Historical Society of Colorado

LITTLE RAVEN AND WILLIAM BENT AT FORT DODGE — 1869
Arapaho Chief Little Raven, his daughter, Colonel William
Bent, and Raven's two sons. The Indian on the far right is
probably the one who led the war party along the Arkansas
during the summer of 1864 when the Snyder group was massacred and Mrs. Snyder taken prisoner.

Shoup to capture another herd which grazed on the back side of the bluffs to the south and west of the village.

The first shot of the battle was fired by Wilson's troops as they drove between the Indian village and the horse herd. His move successful, Wilson swung his command toward the camp, dismounting and taking up positions on the northeast, and began firing into the village.

Anthony and his three Colorado First companies followed across the creek close behind Wilson, pulling up at the southeast of the camp and dismounting, there waiting for Chivington and the Colorado Third to come up and "open the ball." Chivington, meanwhile, halted his remaining force in the bed of the river below the village and ordered the troops to take off their overcoats, yelling to them to "remember the murdered women and children on the Platte!" The Third then moved up, dismounted, and took up positions behind Anthony, commencing a fire over and through Anthony's command.

Baldwin's battery took a position near the creek bank and began lobbing grape and canister at the village, but the shell fell short. Presently the two cannons of the Third went into action, some of their fire landing among the Indians. Cramer, recognizing that his men were in a dangerous position, reported the situation to Anthony, who ordered him to the left along the creek bed, also sending Soule with Company D to the south bank.

McCannon's Company I, reinforced by Captain Baxter with Company G of the Third, was successful in cutting off the Indian herd on the south of the village. A half-dozen Indians, among them George Bent, came running up from the village in an attempt to save the herd, but were driven back to the creek. The herd secured, Companies I and G moved up on the sand bluffs overlooking the village from the south and began firing into the village, establishing a cross-fire dangerous to Wilson's troops who were directly opposite them.

Below them the Cheyenne village was in panic.

On the morning of November 26, the same morning that Wynkoop left for the States, John Smith, who had been ill for some time, left Fort Lyon for the Sand Creek village at the request of Major Anthony. The Fort Lyon commander had called in Smith and asked him to go out to ascertain the number of the Indians on Sand Creek, their disposition toward the whites, and at what points other tribes might be found. Smith agreed readily, as he wanted to go out anyway to do some trading with the Indians. Also, his Indian wife and his son, Jack, were in camp there.

Going along with him was a private of Company G named David Louderback and a teamster, Watson Clark, who was in the employ of Dexter Colley. Driving a wagon loaded with trade goods, the three men arrived at the Cheyenne camp on Sand Creek shortly before noon on the twenty-seventh, finding 115 Cheyenne lodges, plus eight Arapaho lodges under Left Hand pitched below the Cheyennes. The men unloaded their goods in the lodge of War Bonnet, unhitched the mules and turned them loose to graze, and then ate their dinner. That afternoon and during the next day, the twenty-eighth, the goods were traded off for buffalo robes, 104 of them, three ponies, and one mule.

On the morning of the twenty-ninth, the three visitors, along with Jack Smith, rose at daybreak and were eating their breakfast inside a lodge when an Indian woman entered hurriedly and said there was "a heap of buffalo coming." Shortly afterward a Cheyenne chief entered the lodge and said that a big force of soldiers were headed toward camp and wanted Smith to go out and see who they were. Not thinking they would be Fort Lyon troops, Smith and Louderback decided that they must be Blunt's men from Fort Riley, Kansas.

Louderback requested that Jack Smith try to catch him a horse so that he could ride out and see what the troops wanted, but the herd had already been cut off. The crack of gunfire had begun sounding by this time, and Louderback put a white handkerchief on a stick, Smith advancing with it toward the troops. Smith reasoned that he was not to be mistaken for an Indian since he was dressed in a hat, soldier's overcoat, and trousers—very much unlike an Indian. But when he was within 150 yards of the troops, the soldiers began firing on him. Someone yelled, "Shoot the old son of a bitch; he is no better than an Indian."[3]

A soldier named George Pierce, a member of F company attached to Cramer's command, saw Smith's predicament and rode his horse past the lines in an attempt to save him. His horse stumbled and fell, and when Pierce arose he was killed, some say by an Indian and others say is was a soldier's bullet that go him.[4]

Smith and Louderback quickly retreated to the village. After this the teamster Clark secured a lodge pole and tied a tanned buffalo hide onto it, and, standing on the wagon, began waving it at the soldiers. A fusillade of bullets drove him back into the lodge. Louderback remained sitting on the wagon tongue, watching the fight until the howitzer shells

[3] "Sand Creek Massacre," 138.
[4] This is the same George Pierce who, during the Battle of La Glorieta Pass, had dashed forward from his lines to capture a rebel major and captain of the Texas forces.

began bursting around him; he then went to the lodge and stood in the entrance apprehensively watching the battle.

When the attack first began, Black Kettle had quickly remembered the advice given him by the whites on several occasions. In 1860, Greenwood had given him a large American garrison-type flag, and he now tied the flag to the end of a long lodge pole, added a white flag beneath it, and hoisted it above his tent. George Bent tells of Black Kettle's role in the fight:

> When I looked toward the chief's lodge, I saw that Black Kettle had a large American flag up on a long lodgepole as a signal to the troop that the camp was friendly. Part of the people were rushing about the camp in great fear. All the time Black Kettle kept calling out not to be frightened; that the camp was under protection and there was no danger. Then suddenly the troops opened fire on this mass of men, women, and children, and all began to scatter and run. At the beginning of the attack Black Kettle, with his wife and White Antelope, took their position before Black Kettle's lodge and remained there after all others had left the camp. At last Black Kettle, seeing that it was useless to stay longer, started to run. . . .[5]

White Antelope, meanwhile, had run out from the village toward the troops, holding his hands high in the air and yelling at them not to fire. The troops kept coming on, and White Antelope, one of the bravest and greatest of the Cheyenne warriors, stood in the middle of Sand Creek with his arms folded over his chest, hoping to signify by the gesture that the Cheyennes did not wish to fight the whites. The heroic act

[5] Grinnell, *The Fighting Cheyennes*, 177–78.

was wasted on the soldiers, and he was shot down in the bed of the creek.

For a brief time the Cheyenne men had managed a line of defense across the river, but their bows and arrows and few guns were no match for the cavalry fire. It was, perhaps, the thunder of the cannon as much as anything that broke their ranks, turning the village into complete rout. The Indians fled in all directions, but the main body of them moved up the creek bed, which alone offered some protection against the soldiers' bullets. They fled headlong until they came to a place above the camp where the banks of the river were cut back by breaks. Here the Indians frantically began digging in the loose sand with their hands to make holes in which to hide. The larger per cent of these were women and children but the men in the group began fighting desperately from the holes.

During the battle Si Soule had refused to order his men to fire, making it a point that he was opposed to killing the Indians. Keeping his squadron together, he drifted down the south bank of the creek, watching the other troops busily potshooting Indians in the holes and under the river banks.[6]

From the lodge opening, Private Louderback spotted Chivington crossing the creek at the lower end of the village and hallooed to him. Chivington answered, calling Louderback by name and telling him to come on, that he was safe. As Louderback advanced to meet Chivington, however, a soldier fired at him, missing.

[6] Edward E. Wynkoop, "Edward Wanshear Wynkoop," *Kansas State Historical Society*, Vol. XIII, 76–77. Chivington charged that these holes were rifle pits, which in itself indicates how little he actually knew about the Plains Indians. Fortifying a village was unheard of.

I asked the colonel what they were firing at me for, and he turned around and told them to stop firing. He then told me to fall in rear of the command, that I was all right. I told him to hold on a minute, the lodge was full of white men, pointing a lodge out to him in which John Smith was. Just at this time John Smith came out and called Colonel Chivington. Colonel Chivington told him to bring his friends out, that he was all right; he came out, bringing the teamster and Charley Bent, and they fell in with the command.[7]

John Smith attached himself to one of Baldwin's caissons and half-running, half-riding followed along with the soldiers up the stream for over a mile. Here he found a force of about two hundred soldiers had surrounded the Indians who were dug into holes in the creek bed. Smith describes this part of the battle:

By the time I got up with the battery to the place where these Indians were surrounded there had been some considerable firing. Four or five soldiers had been killed, some with arrows and some with bullets. The soldiers continued firing on these Indians, who numbered about a hundred, until they had almost completely destroyed them. I think I saw altogether some seventy dead bodies lying there; the greater portion women and children. There may have been thirty warriors, old and young; the rest were women and small children of different ages and sizes.

The troops at that time were very much scattered. There were not over two hundred troops in the main fight, engaged in killing this body of Indians under the bank. The balance of the troops were scattered in different directions, running after small parties of Indians who were trying to make their escape.[8]

[7] "Sand Creek Massacre," 135.
[8] "Massacre of Cheyenne Indians," 6.

Smith returned to the lodge where his Indian wife and their youngest child had remained throughout the fight. Presently Louderback returned, and a short time later the Indian wife of Charlie Windsor, who had kept the sutler's store at Lyon, was brought in. Shortly afterward Jack Smith, who had at first fled along with Edmund Guerrier, returned to the lodge, having given himself up to Major Sayr. Later in the evening three young Indian children and a papoose about a month old were brought into the lodge.

By three o'clock in the afternoon the fight was over, and the soldiers began straggling back into the village. Then the looting and pillaging became general. Officers and men alike scavenged the Indian camp for souvenirs. Those who had bragged about scalps now lived up to their talk, and much scalping took place.[9]

During the afternoon Anthony ordered Soule to accompany him back to Fort Lyon to escort the supply train from Lyon to the battlefield. Soule went to Chivington to ask permission to take Charles Bent back with him. Chivington at first refused on grounds that Robert Bent did not want his brother taken back, but then he said he guessed he had no objection.

John Smith accompanied Lieutenant Colonel Bowen over the field to identify the dead, and he mistook a badly cut up body for that of Black Kettle. Among the dead he found the body of One-Eye.

[9] In addition, fingers and ears were cut off the bodies for the jewelry they carried. The body of White Antelope, lying solitarily in the creek bed, was a prime target. Besides scalping him the soldiers cut off his nose, ears, and testicles—the last for a tobacco pouch supposedly. Some of the men later tried to lay the blame for this on Lieutenant Autobees' Company H Mexican troops, but there is much evidence that Major Sayr and Lieutenant Richmond were guilty as well as many of the other troops. See the Appendix in regard to exact testimony concerning atrocities at Sand Creek.

That night the troops made camp on the battlefield, the men sleeping on their guns despite a heavy guard posted. Twice during the night an alarm sounded and sporadic firing broke out among the jittery soldiers. The same evening Chivington exultingly wrote a dispatch to General Curtis reporting on the battle:

> In the last ten days my command has marched 300 miles, 100 of which the snow was two feet deep. After a march of forty miles last night I, at daylight this morning, attacked Cheyenne village of 130 lodges, from 900 to 1,000 warriors strong; killed Chiefs Black Kettle, White Antelope, Knock Knee, and Little Robe [Little Raven], and between 400 and 500 other Indians, and captured as many ponies and mules. Our loss [was] 9 killed, 38 wounded. All did nobly. Think I will catch some more of them eighty miles, on Smoky Hill. Found white man's scalp, not more than three days' old, in one of lodges.[10]

At the same time he dispatched a messenger to Denver with a letter to the editor of the *Rocky Mountain News*, telling of his victory in "one of the most bloody Indian battles ever fought on these plains." He stated: "I shall leave here, as soon as I can see our wounded safely on the way to the hospital at Fort Lyon, for the villages of the Sioux, which are reported

[10] *Rebellion Records*, Series I, Vol. XLI, Part I, 948; "The Chivington Massacre," 91.

Grinnell, in *The Fighting Cheyennes*, 167, lists these chiefs as being killed at Sand Creek: White Antelope, Standing in the Water, One-Eye, War Bonnet, Spotted Crow, Two Thighs, Bear Man, Yellow Shield, Yellow Wolf, and Left Hand. This list is probably nearly correct, though Left Hand was not killed and lived to be an old man, despite confusing statements by Ed Guerrier, Bent, Colley, and even Little Raven that Left Hand was done in at Sand Creek. No-ta-ne (Knock Knee) was evidently killed as Chivington reported.

80 miles from here on the Smoky Hill, and three thousand strong; so look for more fighting."[11]

Private Louderback cooked supper that night and breakfast the next morning for the Indian prisoners. During the morning of the thirtieth, some soldiers appeared at the lodge and said that Chivington had ordered them to take all the robes, blankets, and provisions for the hospital. John Smith went to Chivington and complained about the matter, and Shoup placed guards on the prisoners' tent. The guards stayed there until about noon that day, then left and did not come back again.

Meanwhile a great deal of talk concerning Jack Smith had been circulating among the soldiers, who were threatening to kill him. When Chivington was informed that the soldiers were likely to kill Jack, he replied that he had given orders to take no prisoners and he had no new instructions now.[12]

[11] *Rebellion Records,* Series I, Vol. XLI, Part I, 950–51; "Massacre of Cheyenne Indians," 48.

[12] In his testimony Soule stated, "I heard Lieutenant Dunn ask Colonel Chivington if he had any objections to having Jack Smith killed. Colonel Chivington said that he need not ask him about it; he knew how he (Chivington) felt about it, or words to that effect." "Sand Creek Massacre," 28.

Anthony testified, "I went to Colonel Chivington and told him that Jack Smith was a man he might make very useful to him; that he could be made a good guide or scout for us; 'but,' said I to him, 'unless you give your men to understand that you want the man saved, he is going to be killed. He will be killed before tomorrow morning, unless you give your men to understand that you don't want him killed.' Colonel Chivington replied, 'I have given my instructions; have told my men not to take any prisoners.'" "Massacre of Cheyenne Indians," 22.

Shoup said, "I heard him [Chivington] say we must not allow John Smith and family, father of Jack Smith, to be harmed; that he did not intend to take any Indians prisoners." "Sand Creek Massacre," 177.

John Smith testified, "He [Jack] came in quietly and sat down; he remained there [in the lodge] that day, that night, and the next day in the afternoon; about four o'clock in the evening, as I was sitting inside the camp, a soldier

That afternoon ten to fifteen men, some of them Dunn's men, entered the lodge where the Indian prisoners were being held. Louderback described the affair:

> In the afternoon there were several men in talking to Jack Smith, and told him he was a son of a bitch, and ought to have been shot long ago. Jack told the man that was talking to him that he did not give a damn; that if he wanted to kill him, shoot him. When Jack said this I thought it was time for me to get out of there, as men had threatened to hang and shoot me as well as uncle John Smith and the teamster that was with us.[13]

Old Jim Beckwith was there, and he described what happened then:

came up outside of the lodge and called me by name. I got up and went out; he took me by the arm and walked towards Colonel Chivington's camp, which was about sixty yards from my camp. Said he, 'I am sorry to tell you, but they are going to kill your son Jack.' I knew the feeling towards the whole camp of Indians, and that there was no use to make any resistance. I said, 'I can't help it.' I then walked on towards where Colonel Chivington was standing by his camp-fire; when I had got within a few feet of him I heard a gun fired, and saw a crowd run to my lodge, and they told me that Jack was dead. . . . Major Anthony, who was present, told Colonel Chivington that he had heard some remarks made, indicating that they were desirous of killing Jack; and that he (Colonel Chivington) had it in his power to save him, and that by saving him he might make him a very useful man, as he was well acquainted with all the Cheyenne and Arapahoe country, and he could be used as a guide or interpreter. Colonel Chivington replied to Major Anthony, as the Major himself told me, that he had no orders to receive and no advice to give." "Massacre of Cheyenne Indians," 10.

In a letter to his brother Major Anthony wrote, "We, of course, took no prisoners, except John Smith's son, and he was taken suddenly ill in the night, and died before morning." "The Chivington Massacre," 92.

Major Sayr tried to say that Jack Smith was killed accidentally when looking at a gun, but he admits that "some of the boys dragged the body out onto the prairie and hauled it about for a considerable time." Hal Sayre, "Early Central City Theatrical and Other Reminiscences," *The Colorado Magazine,* Vol. VI (1929), 47–53. During his early years in Colorado Major Sayr spelled his name "Sayr," later changing it to "Sayre."

He [Jack Smith] was sitting in the lodge with me; not more than five or six feet from me, just across the lodge. There were from ten to fifteen soldiers came into the lodge at the time, and there was some person came on the outside and called to his father, John Smith. He, the old man, went out, and there was a pistol fired when the old man got out of the lodge. There was a piece of the lodge cut out where [when] the old man went out. There was a pistol fired through this opening and the bullet entered below his [Jack Smith's] right breast. He sprung forward and fell dead, and the lodge scattered, soldiers, squaws, and everything else. I went out myself; as I went out I met a man with a pistol in his hand. He made this remark to me: he said, "I am afraid the damn son of a bitch is not dead, and I will finish him." Says I, "Let him go to rest; he is dead." . . . We took him out and laid him out of doors. I do not know what they did with him afterwards.[14]

Louderback, meanwhile, had just reached Colonel Chivington's headquarters when the report of the pistol was heard. Chivington, upon hearing the shot, said, "Halloo. I wonder what that is."

I answered by saying that they had shot Jack Smith, and I thought it was a damned shame the way that they killed him. No matter what a man had done, they ought to give him a show for his life. Upon which some officer—I could not name him, I do not know what his name is—told me I had better be careful how I "shot my mouth off" around there about killing Indians. I told him I enlisted as a soldier, and I considered my tongue my own; that I did not consider that it belonged to the government; that I thought I could use it whenever I wanted to. Sergeant Palmer, of our company, was standing near me at the time. He told me I had better go down and stay with the company, or I would get shot yet before I left the village. I

13 "Sand Creek Massacre," 136.
14 *Ibid.*, 71.

told him they could have a chance to shoot me in a few days, as soon as I could go to the fort and back, as I did not have anything to shoot with now.[15]

Some skirmishing continued during the day of the thirtieth, and a few more Indians were killed. The transportation arrived from Fort Lyon that day, and Lieutenant Cramer was ordered to burn the Cheyenne village. He complied with the order, and Black Kettle's village was put to the torch. The troops again slept on their weapons that night.

In his report to Colonel Shoup written that night, Lieutenant Colonel Bowen sent congratulations on "the signal punishment meted out to the savages on yesterday, 'who so ruthlessly have murdered our women and children,' in the language of the colonel commanding, although I regret the loss of so many brave men. The third regiment cannot any longer be called the 'bloodless third.' "[16]

And Captain Cree, of the Colorado Third, prophetically wrote, "All I can say for officers and men is, that they all behaved well, and won for themselves a name that will be remembered for ages to come."[17]

At about nine o'clock on the morning of December 1, Chivington's force fell into formation and marched; not, however, toward the Smoky Hill, but in the opposite direction southward toward the Arkansas where it was reported that Little

[15] *Ibid.*, 136.
[16] "Massacre of Cheyenne Indians," 52. Bowen also stated, "The war flag of this band of Cheyennes is in my possession, presented by Stephen Decatur, commissary sergeant of company C, who acted as my battalion adjutant."

In his testimony ("Sand Creek Massacre," 200) Decatur said much of his seeing no white flag during the battle but avoids any mention of the "war flag," which evidently was the United States flag raised by Black Kettle.
[17] "Massacre of Cheyenne Indians," 53.

Raven and his less formidable band of Arapahoes were camped. The soldiers camped that night in the dry bed of Sand Creek, fifteen miles south of the battlefield. From here the wounded and dead were sent into Fort Lyon, the first to be cared for, Chivington said, and "the latter to be buried on our own soil."[18] It was here, also, that Anthony and Soule rejoined the command with the supply train.

On the next day the troops marched to the mouth of Sand Creek where they went into camp until eleven o'clock that night, at which time Chivington gave hurried marching orders to overtake the Indians reported down-river. The command marched all night, traveling forty-two miles and crossing the Kansas border to reach a camp site of the Arapahoes, finding the Indians gone. Chivington halted here and waited for his transportation to catch up, sending Soule with twenty men out to scout for Indians and look out for a wagon train which was on the Aubrey branch of the Santa Fe road headed for Santa Fe.

On the morning of December 4, a stagecoach[19] came up the river and met the expedition, reporting an encampment of Indians some fifteen miles below. Sending Shoup with thirty men to the south bank, Chivington continued down the north side, only to find once again that the Arapahoes had slipped away. That night the two units went into camp across the Arkansas from one another. Crossing back over the next morning, Shoup found that Chivington had already taken a small command out on a scout. When he returned around ten o'clock that morning, the command was again put in motion, travel-

[18] *Ibid.*, 49.
[19] This was the stage carrying Julia Lambert which met Wynkoop at Fort Larned.

ing some twelve miles farther down the river. Again, the Indians were gone.

Chivington's army lay in camp the rest of the day, December 5, sending a scout about twenty miles in a northeasterly direction. It returned without having sighted any Indians. Discouraged, Chivington called a consultation of his officers, and it was agreed that since their horses were giving out it was impracticable to pursue Little Raven any farther. It was also agreed that a hunting trip to the Smoky Hill and Republican was not too good an idea. Thus, on December 7, the weather cold and clear, Chivington broke camp and headed back up the Arkansas, reaching Fort Lyon on the tenth.

Here he learned that Lieutenant Hewitt, Company I, Third Colorado, had arrested Duncan McKeith and four Mexicans of Lieutenant Autobees' company and taken into custody some fifty to sixty head of Cheyenne ponies and mules which had been driven away from Sand Creek even while the battle was in progress. These had been taken to Autobees' ranch, across the river from Boone's place, and discovered by Hewitt, who took them with him to Lyon. Another herd had been driven off toward the Cimarron country.[20]

The Colorado Third troops arrived in Denver on December 22, where they paraded down the streets led by Chivington with a live eagle tied to a pole. The *News* reported, "Headed by the First Regiment band, and by Colonels Chivington and

[20] "Sand Creek Massacre," 201.

George W. Thompson wrote that he was in the Fort Lyon vicinity after the battle and went to Colonel Chivington's tent where he bought fifteen head of horses at twenty-five dollars each. "Experiences in the West," *The Colorado Magazine,* Vol. IV (1927), 175–79. Autobees claimed Chivington had known he was taking the horses. When Lieutenant Hewitt turned up at Lyon with them, Chivington said he had instructed Autobees to drive them to the fort.

Shoup, Lieut. Col. Bowen and Major Sayr, the rank and file of the 'bloody Thirdsters' made a most imposing procession, extending, with the transportation trains, from the upper end of Ferry street, through Latimer, G and Blake, almost back to Ferry street again. As the 'bold sojer boys' passed along, the sidewalks and corner stands were thronged with citizens saluting their old friends."[21]

On December 25, 1864, Major Sayr entered in his diary: "In Camp—None of our Regiment mustered out yet—Some of the boys trying to have a Merry Christmas by getting drunk."[22] Three days later the Third Regiment of the Colorado Volunteers was mustered out of the service.

Chivington, having ridden ahead of the troops, reported to General Curtis from Denver on December 16, giving a full account of his march and the battle, stating: "It may perhaps be unnecessary for me to state that I captured no prisoners." He continued: "I cannot conclude this report without saying that the conduct of Capt. Silas S. Soule, Company D, First Cavalry of Colorado, was at least ill-advised, he saying that he thanked God he had killed no Indians, and like expressions, proving him more in sympathy with those Indians than with the whites."[23]

Chivington then found it necessary to defend his actions by claiming to have found "several scalps of white men and women in the Indian lodges; also various articles of clothing

[21] *Rocky Mountain News,* Denver, December 22, 1864.

[22] Lynn I. Perrigo, "Major Hal Sayre's Diary of the Sand Creek Campaign," *The Colorado Magazine,* Vol. XV (1938), 41–57. On December 23, 1864, the *News* reported: "Our streets, hotels, saloons and stores to-day were thronged with strangers, chiefly 'Indian killers.' A high old time there was last night, around."

[23] *Rebellion Records,* Series I, Vol. XLI, Part I, 948–50.

belonging to white persons." "On every hand the evidence was clear," he wrote, "that no lick was struck amiss."

The *Rocky Mountain News* reported the affair with great praise, "Among the brilliant feats of arms in Indian warfare, the recent campaign of our Colorado Volunteers will stand in history with few rivals, and none to exceed it in final results. . . . A thousand incidents of individual daring and the passing events of the day might be told, but space forbids. We leave the task for eye-witnesses to chronicle. All acquitted themselves well, and Colorado soldiers have again covered themserves with glory."[24]

[24] *Rocky Mountain News*, December 17, 1864.

X.

RECRIMINATIONS
AND
INVESTIGATIONS

REPERCUSSIONS OF THE SAND CREEK AFFAIR were quick to be heard. Word of it had reached Washington, D. C., and in late December the *News* printed a dispatch from the capitol, dated December 20, 1864, "The affair at Fort Lyon, Colorado, in which Colonel Chivington destroyed a large Indian village, and all its inhabitants, is to be made the subject of congressional investigation. Letters received from high officials in Colorado say that the Indians were killed after surrendering, and that a large proportion of them were women and children."[1]

Denver citizens, especially the men of the Third, expressed their indignation loudly, and there was talk of "going for"

[1] *Rocky Mountain News,* Denver, December 29, 1864, p. 2.

those "high officials."[2] The *News* took up the defense of Chivington and the "boys of the Third" passionately, claiming that the Indians killed were the "confessed murderers of the Hungate family."

"It is unquestioned and undenied," wrote the *News*, "that the site of the Sand creek battle was the rendezvous of the thieving and marauding bands of savages who roamed over this country last summer and fall, and it is shrewdly suspected that somebody was all the time making a very good thing of it."[3]

Matters moved quickly after the first of the year. Wynkoop, now at Fort Riley, had gone "wild with rage" upon hearing of the massacre. On December 31, 1864, he was ordered back to Lyon to take command of the post again and "to make thorough investigation of recent operations against the Indians and make a detailed report."[4] He arrived at Fort Lyon on January 14, 1865, and immediately began taking testimony and affidavits from persons there: Smith, Cannon, Minton, Louderback and Clark, and Colley. On the fifteenth he wrote a scathing report to district headquarters, which was forwarded through channels to Washington, in which he called Chivington an "inhuman monster." He accompanied the report with the affidavits, all of which denounced the attack.[5]

---

[2] *Ibid.*, December 30, 1864. The high official was later disclosed to be Chief Justice of Colorado Benjamin Hall. Many figured it to be Tappan and there was talk of stringing him up. Colley, also, had written to Senator Doolittle of Wisconsin concerning the massacre.

[3] *Ibid.*

[4] *Rebellion Records,* Series I, Vol. XLI, Part IV, 971.

[5] *Ibid.*, Part I, 959–62.
When Wynkoop returned to Fort Lyon, he also immediately began fortifying the hill position of Bent's New Fort, in use as a commissary, for protec-

On January 10, 1865, the House of Representatives passed the motion "That the Committee on the Conduct of the War be required to inquire into and report all the facts connected with the late attack of the third regiment of Colorado volunteers, under Colonel Chivington, on a village of the Cheyenne tribe of Indians, near Fort Lyon."[6] From March 13 through March 15 this congressional group heard testimony relative to the massacre. Governor Evans, already in Washington, D. C., was called in to testify. Also called was Jesse Leavenworth. A party from Fort Lyon and Denver included John Smith, Major Anthony, Major Colley and his son, Captain S. M. Robbins of the Colorado First, and United States Marshal Hunt. The committee compiled affidavits, correspondence, and official reports relative to what they titled "Massacre of Cheyenne Indians." At the last of this compilation is testimony in which Chivington answered at length in Denver questions put to him by the committee. Chivington claimed that he was told by Anthony and Colley that the Indians at Sand Creek were hostile, that though Wynkoop had offered them protection Anthony had driven them from the post. He stated that when he arrived at Lyon he "heard nothing of the recent statement that the Indians were under the protection

tion of the women and children against the expected retaliatory war by the Indians. *Rocky Mountain News,* January 27, 1865.

He threw up breastworks on the north and east of the Bent building and built a stone wall covering the road to the river, to prevent the place being cut off from water. Cannons were mounted on the northeast and northwest corners. "Every man in the Fort worked on the breastworks except the officer of the day and the guard. Major Wynkoop, in a blue flannel shirt, used pick or shovel as it was needed and everybody worked hard to complete the fortifications." Julia S. Lambert, "Plain Tales of the Plains," *The Trail,* Vol. VIII (1916), No. 13, 16.

[6] "Massacre of Cheyenne Indians," i.

of the government. . . ." There were in the Indian camp, he said, some eleven or twelve hundred Indians, of which seven hundred were warriors, and the white scalp which he had claimed finding on the day of the battle had now multiplied. "We found in the camp the scalps of nineteen (19) white persons."[7]

The conclusion of the committee was extremely censorious of Evans:

> His [Evans'] testimony before your committee was characterized by such prevarication and shuffling as has been shown by no witness they have examined during the four years they have been engaged in their investigations; and for the evident purpose of avoiding the admission that he was fully aware that the Indians massacred so brutally at Sand Creek, were then, and had been, actuated by the most friendly feelings towards the whites, and had done all in their power to restrain those less friendly disposed.[8]

Anthony admitted to the committee that he had told the Indians: ". . . I could make no offers of peace to them until I heard from district headquarters. I told them, however, that they might go out and camp on Sand creek, and remain there

[7] *Ibid.*, 104

[8] *Ibid.*, iv.

Evans made a lengthy reply to the committee charges. This document appears in "The Chivington Massacre," 77–87. In it Evans contended: (1) That the white prisoners had been captured, not purchased, by the Cheyennes, as claimed by the committee. (2) That the Indians had been hostile and committed acts of hostility. (3) That he had not sent the Indians to Fort Lyon, that he had turned them over to the jurisdiction of the military. (4) That he had tried diligently to prevent hostilities. (5) That he had not lied to the committee. Reverend Oliver Williard of the Methodist Episcopal Church in Denver, of which both Evans and Chivington were members, swore that Chivington had several times told him that Evans had no knowledge of the expedition and knew nothing about it. *Ibid.*, 70.

if they chose to do so; but they should not camp in the vicinity of the post; and if I had authority to make peace with them I would go out and let them know of it."[9] Anthony also stated that he did not approve of Chivington's attacking the camp.

Of him the committee was more condemnatory:

The testimony of Major Anthony, who succeeded an officer disposed to treat these Indians with justice and humanity, is sufficient of itself to show how unprovoked and unwarranted was this massacre. He testifies that he found these Indians in the neighborhood of Fort Lyon when he assumed command of that post; that they professed their friendliness to the whites, and their willingness to do whatever he demanded of them; that they delivered their arms up to him; that they went to and encamped upon the place designated by him; that they gave him information from time to time of acts of hostility which were meditated by other and hostile bands, and in every way conducted themselves properly and peaceably, and yet he says it was fear and not principle which prevented his killing them while they were completely in his power. And when Colonel Chivington appeared at Fort Lyon, on his mission of murder and barbarity, Major Anthony made haste to accompany him with men and artillery, although Colonel Chivington had no authority whatever over him.[10]

[9] "Massacre of Cheyenne Indians," 18.

Upon arriving back at Fort Lyon on December 15, Anthony immediately reported to Fort Riley: "I am of the (same) opinion that I was when reporting on the 25th November. I then thought that it would not be policy to fight these Indians who were suing for peace until they were completely humbled. . . . I am of the opinion now that the road and the settlements above us are in worse condition than before the arrival of Colonel Chivington's command. . . . I think one such visitation to each hostile tribe would forever put an end to Indian war on the plains, and I regret exceedingly that this punishment could not have fallen upon some other band." *Rebellion Records,* Series I, Vol. XLI, Part I, 953–54.

[10] "Massacre of Cheyenne Indians," iv–v.

But it was Chivington whom the committee found to be the real villain:

> As to Colonel Chivington, your committee can hardly find fitting terms to describe his conduct. Wearing the uniform of the United States, which should be the emblem of justice and humanity; holding the important position of commander of a military district, and therefore having the honor of the government to that extent in his keeping, he deliberately planned and executed a foul and dastardly massacre which would have disgraced the veriest savage among those who were the victims of his cruelty.[11]

At the same time of this investigation by the Committee on the Conduct of the War, another congressional inquiry was under way, this one by a Joint Special Committee of the two houses of Congress, a committee already established for the purpose of investigating the condition of all the western Indian tribes and their treatment by civil and military authorities. This committee was divided into three groups by geographical category, and to Congressmen Foster, Doolittle, and Ross was assigned the duty of investigating the areas of Kansas, the Indian Nation, and the territories of Colorado, New Mexico, and Utah.[12]

On March 7 and 8 testimony was taken by this group in Washington from Colley, Leavenworth, Smith, and Evans. The committee then traveled west, stopping at Fort Riley, where they took affidavits, including one from Edmund Guerrier; on to Larned, where they talked with Colonel Ford of the Second Colorado Regiment, in command there, and an

[11] *Ibid.*, v.
[12] *Report of the Joint Special Committee Appointed under Resolution of March 3, 1865*, Appendix, 3.

Indian trader named Dodds; then on to Fort Lyon, where on June 9 they took direct testimony from Wynkoop, William Bent, and Robert Bent. The congressmen also went to Santa Fe, where they talked with the famous Kit Carson, and to Denver, where they interviewed Downing and others. This committee concluded, ". . . But the fact which gives such terrible force to the condemnation of the wholesale massacre of Arrapahoes and Cheyennes, by the Colorado troops under Colonel Chivington, near Fort Lyon, was, that those Indians were there encamped under the direction of our own officers, and believed themselves to be under the protection of our flag."[13]

The most thorough and dramatic investigation of the Sand Creek Massacre, however, took place in Colorado under the direction of the army. On February 1, 1865, a military commission was ordered for the purpose of investigating "the conduct of the late Colonel J. M. Chivington, first regiment Colorado cavalry, in his recent campaign against the Indians."[14]

Several changes had taken place in the military setup of Colorado: Chivington had resigned his commission on January 4 and was mustered out of the service on the eighth, being replaced in command of the district by Colonel Tom Moonlight.[15] Both Tappan and Wynkoop claimed that Chivington's commission had already expired prior to the Sand Creek Massacre. Tappan wrote, "Col. Chivington's term in the army expired 23rd September 1864 though he continued in command until Jan. 6, 1865, and is not liable to be tried for such crimes as these by a military court."[16]

[13] *Ibid.*, 5–6.
[14] "Sand Creek Massacre," 2.
[15] *Rebellion Records*, Series I, Vol. XLVIII, Part I, 416.
[16] Paper by Samuel F. Tappan, Kansas State Historical Society.

Anthony resigned his commission on January 21.

Moonlight detailed Tappan, Captain Ed Jacobs, and Captain George Stilwell as members of the commission to ascertain whether or not civilized rules of warfare were followed at Sand Creek, whether or not the Indians were under the protection of the government, whether or not they were in open hostility, and whether or not Chivington had taken proper steps to prevent "unnatural outrages." The commission was also called on to look into the matter of prisoners, their treatment, and the disposition of government property, such as the horses and mules used.[17]

Moonlight specified that this was not intended as a trial of any person, but the purpose was simply to investigate and accumulate facts to fix the responsibility of the fight. Chivington was allowed legal assistance and the privilege of cross-examination.

Tappan's presence on the board was fought bitterly by Chivington, who claimed him to be an "open and avowed enemy" who expressed himself as being very much prejudiced against the killing of the Sand Creek Indians and, further, that Tappan did not have the character to divest himself of his prejudices in the matter.[18] Tappan admitted to his remarks of opposition to the massacre, but maintained that the alleged prejudices, even if true, would not hamper him in carrying out his duties.[19] One way or another, Tappan remained as chairman of the committee.

The first witness, appearing before the committee on February 11, was Silas Soule, who testified at length in answer

[17] "Sand Creek Massacre," 3-4.
[18] Ibid., 5.
[19] Ibid., 8.

to questions by the commission for two days, was cross-examined by Chivington and his counsel for four days, and then reexamined by the Commissioner and Chivington for another day.[20] He was followed on the stand by Cramer and several other witnesses until March 10 when the commission adjourned to Fort Lyon, where they reconvened on March 20. Here Wynkoop, Prowers, Cannon, Cossitt, Louderback, and several others testified at length until the commission returned to Denver on April 8.

Shortly after the proceedings had once more gotten under way in Denver, an event took place which brought them to a temporary halt. Though the public had not been allowed in to the hearings, the word had "gotten around" Denver as to what transpired each day. There was much talk against those in opposition to the Sand Creek affair, especially against the outspoken Soule, now provost marshal of Denver, who had been the first to testify. Threats had been made against him, and several shots fired upon him from ambush were proof that the threats were not idle ones.[21]

Notwithstanding the danger of his situation, Soule proceeded to be married on April 1, 1865, in Denver, the *News* commenting that Soule and his wife had set up housekeeping on Curtis Street "where is is expected that the name of Soule will succeed, spread and flourish like the branches of a green

[20] *Ibid.,* 8–29.

[21] *Ibid.,* 188–89.

Captain George F. Price, district inspector and Acting Assistant Adjutant General in Denver, swore in his deposition that in the latter part of March he and Soule had traveled together to Central City and Soule had said then that he fully expected to be killed for his part in the hearings and that an attempt would be made to blacken his character afterward to nullify his testimony before the commission. *Ibid.,* 189.

bay tree."[22] It was less than a month later, on the twenty-third, that Soule, having just returned home with his wife from visiting a friend, heard the sound of shots. Grabbing his gun, he ran from his house up Lawrence Street toward the gunfire. It was near F Street that he was met by a man, a soldier of the Colorado Second named Squiers, who was waiting for him with a gun. The two men fired simultaneously. Squiers' ball hit Soule in the cheek, and the former Kansas jayhawker fell dead. Squiers, hit in the right arm, dropped his gun and ran into the night, leaving a trail of blood behind him.[23]

Soule was buried three days later, the *News* reporting, "The funeral of the late Capt. Silas S. Soule, Provost Marshal, took place yesterday noon and was attended by an unusually large and respectable procession. . . . A long line of carriages—almost all the public and private ones in town."[24]

Squiers fled to New Mexico, where in Las Vegas he was spotted by two men who recognized him and notified Lieutenant Cannon of the New Mexico Volunteers. Cannon made the arrest and took Squiers back to Denver, where he turned the man over to the military authorities for court-martial trial.[25] On July 14, Lieutenant Cannon was found mysteriously dead in his room at the Tremont House.[26] It was suspected he had been poisoned, though no proof of this was ever established. Squiers again escaped and reportedly headed for California.

When the military investigation resumed on the day after Soule's funeral, Chivington was allowed to call forth his wit-

[22] *Rocky Mountain News,* April 14, 1865.
[23] *Ibid.,* April 24, 1865, p. 2.
[24] *Ibid.,* April 27, 1865.
[25] *Ibid.,* July 12, 1865.
[26] *Ibid.,* July 15, 1865.

nesses and present his evidence. One of his first acts was to present a deposition taken before a notary public on April 7 preceding.[27] This deposition of a freighter named Lipman Meyer, who had accompanied Soule on his scout near Camp Wynkoop during Chivington's pursuit of Little Raven down the Arkansas after the massacre, had no bearing on the inquiry other than to make Soule out to be a coward, a drunkard, and a thief. Meyer claimed that during the scout Soule had been so drunk that he did not know one direction from another, that he had refused to investigate a supposed Indian camp because he was afraid to fight Indians, and that he and Cannon had stolen some blankets from Meyer.

Among those called in by Chivington to testify in his behalf were Dunn, Cree, Talbot, Richmond, Johnson, and several other Colorado Third officers. Through them Chivington sought to establish that (1) the Indians were hostile by virtue of their having prepared rifle pits, (2) that the Indians were guilty of depredations as proved by white scalps found in their village, and (3) that Soule, Smith, and Colley and other traders were in cahoots with the Indians and were profiting from their war against the whites.[28]

The proceedings continued until May 30, 1865, and after Chivington had declared that he had no more witnesses to present for the defense, the commission stood adjourned. This had been a fact-finding affair and the commission drew no conclusions to the testimony and had no power to make any recommendations. No action was taken against Chivington by this group or by either of the congressional committees.

[27] "Sand Creek Massacre," 184–87.

[28] The matter of atrocities and scalpings by the white soldiers was mostly avoided with witnesses introduced by Chivington.

No longer would the lodges of the Southern Cheyenne and Arapaho tribes be camped along the Arkansas. But in the months to follow, the vengeance of the Cheyennes would be done. Along the Platte and in the northern tier of Plains states, the Dog Soldiers and most of the young men of the tribes, including George and Charlie Bent, would join in with the Sioux and the northern bands of the Cheyennes and Arapahoes in a vicious, bloody war against whites who knew nothing of Lean Bear's killing or how the massacre at Sand Creek came about.

Black Kettle, holding on to the wisdom of old Chief Yellow Wolf, would take the remnant of his band south of the Arkansas, continuing to travel the path of peace with the whites, despite the mortification and doubts which beset him. At the Treaty of the Little Arkansas in the fall of 1865, Black Kettle spoke of Sand Creek, ". . . my shame is as big as the earth. . . . I once thought that I was the only man that persevered to be the friend of the white man, but since they have come and cleaned out our lodges, horses, and everything else, it is hard for me to believe the white man any more. . . ."[29]

At the great Medicine Lodge Treaty of 1867, many of those who had played a part in the Colorado drama would meet again—Tappan, Wynkoop, Boone, Leavenworth, George and Charlie Bent, Smith, Black Kettle, Little Raven, Bull Bear, and others. But the road of peace with the white man still led to disaster. On November 27, 1868, almost four years to the day after Sand Creek, Black Kettle's camp on the Washita in Indian Territory would again be attacked in the cold dawn, this time by Custer and his Seventh Cavalry. Here Black Kettle, the great peacemaker chief of the Cheyennes, would be killed.

29 *Annual Report* of the Commissioner of Indian Affairs, 1865, 704.

After Sand Creek, the glory days of the once-proud Colorado First Regiment were ended. The conglomerate of eager
Americans who had come to Colorado for gold and won honor
on the battlefield were now split with dissension. The enormous *esprit de corps* that had been welded together by the
rattle of musket fire and the acid smell of burnt powder at La
Glorieta was shattered by the moral dispute over Chivington's
massacre at Sand Creek.

Soule was dead, and with the end of the Civil War, most of
the men and officers were mustered out of the service. For
Brevet-Colonel Tappan,[30] as a member of the government's
Peace Commission, and Brevet-Lieutenant Colonel Wynkoop, as agent of the Cheyenne and Arapaho tribes, there
would remain the frustration of helping to steer a course
through the times of Indian difficulties to follow.

William Bent, his day ended with finality at Sand Creek,
would die of pneumonia on May 19, 1869. Charlie Bent, dis-
owned by his father, had already died of Pawnee wounds and
malaria in a Cheyenne war camp. Robert would live until 1889.
George Bent, after fighting for a time with the Dog Soldiers,
would follow the Cheyennes to Oklahoma and their agency
there, imparting to writers and scholars much history of the
Cheyenne that would have otherwise been lost.

John Smith would continue to serve as a scout and interpreter for the army, finally reaching the end of his long and
vigorous trail near the Cheyenne and Arapaho Agency in
Oklahoma in June of 1871. Colonel Boone would also follow
the tribe to Indian Territory, later becoming an agent for the
Kiowas and Comanches. Major Colley, removed from his post,

[30] Tappan adopted an Indian girl orphaned at Sand Creek. She died while
attending a New York girls' school, where she was an excellent student.

would return to his native Wisconsin. Governor Evans would move on into the future with Colorado, successful both politically and financially. Shoup would later become governor of Idaho Territory; Downing, a Colorado millionaire.

For John Chivington there would remain a long and empty life, leaving Colorado for California, thence to Cincinnati, returning to Denver in 1883, where he made a speech at a celebration of the Denver Pike's Peak Pioneers and impassionately justified the Sand Creek attack. The account of the one white scalp which Chivington found in the Sand Creek village had again grown with the years:

"What of that Indian blanket," he asked, "that was captured, fringed with white women's scalps? What says the sleeping dust of the two hundred and eight men, women, and children, emigrants, herders, and soldiers who lost their lives at the hands of these Indians? I say here, as I said in a speech one night last week—I stand by Sand Creek."[31]

The great prestige he had once enjoyed and which had promised so much for him was now gone. Chivington's page in history, rightfully earned at La Glorieta, had been nullified by the massacre at Sand Creek.

Today the site of the massacre reveals little of interest. Cottonwood and willow still mark the bend of Sand Creek, a faint trickle of water still wends along the sandy bed. A near century has brought but slight change to Chivington's punishment grounds of the Cheyenne. Only a rueful emptiness hangs there where a Cheyenne band once camped in peace and was struck down.

[31] William M. Thayer, *Marvels of the New West*, 246.

APPENDIX

Testimony and affidavits concerning the number of Indians killed at Sand Creek, the question of flags, white scalps found in the Indian camp, and atrocities committed by the soldiers.

Samuel G. Colley, Indian Agent

The Chivington Massacre, Testimony, p. 29—I can state according to the received version, that the command marched at 8 o'clock in the evening from Fort Lyon. They attacked the village, which was 30 miles distant, and fired into it about day-light. The Indians, for a while, made some resistance. Some of the chiefs did not lift an arm, but stood there and were shot down. One of them, Black Kettle, raised the American flag, and raised a white flag. He was supposed to be killed, but was not. They retreated right up the creek. They were followed up and pursued and killed and butchered. None denied that they were butchered in a brutal manner and scalped and mutilated as bad as an Indian ever did to a white man. That is admitted by the parties who did it. They were cut to pieces in almost every manner and form. . . .

He [Ed Guerrier] rode with them to the camp and was with them 14 days after they got together on Smoky Hill. He said there were 148 missing when they got in. After that quite a number came in; I cannot tell how many. There were eight who came into Fort Lyon to us, reducing it down to about 130 missing, according to the last information I had. . . .

The officers told me they killed and butchered all they came to. They saw little papooses killed by the soldiers. Colonel Shupe was in command of the regiment; Colonel Chivington in command of the whole force.

The Chivington Massacre, Affidavit, January 27, 1865, p. 52— . . . Colonel Chivington did, on the morning of the 29th of November last, surprise and attack said camp of friendly Indians and massacre a large number of them, (mostly women and children,) and did allow the troops of his command to mangle and mutilate them in the most horrible manner.

D. D. COLLEY, TRADER

Massacre of Cheyenne Indians, Testimony, p. 16—I should judge there were between 100 and 150. What I judge from is this: the inspector of the district went with me to Fort Lyon, and he went out to the battle-field. The bodies were lying there then. They spent half a day on the battle-field, and found 69 bodies. . . .

The inspector told me that about three-fourths of them were women and children.

JOHN S. SMITH, INTERPRETER

The Chivington Massacre, Testimony, p. 42—I think about seventy or eighty, including men, women, and children, were killed; twenty-five or thirty of them were warriors probably, and the rest women, children, boys, and old men.

[The Indian barbarities practiced were] The worst I have ever seen.

All manner of depredations were inflicted on their persons; they were scalped, their brains knocked out; the men used their knives, ripped open women, clubbed little children, knocked them in the head with their guns, beat their brains out, mutilated their bodies in every sense of the word.

It would be hard for me to tell who did these things: I saw some of the first Colorado regiment committing some very bad acts there on the persons of the Indians, and I likewise saw some of the one-hundred-day men in the same kind of business.

The Chivington Massacre, Affidavit, January 15, 1865, p. 51—When the troops began approaching, I saw Black Kettle, the head chief, hoist the American flag, fearing there might be some mistake as to who they were.

Massacre of Cheyenne Indians, Testimony, p. 9—I saw the bodies of those lying there cut all to pieces, worse mutilated than any I ever saw before, the women cut all to pieces.

[They were cut] With knives; scalped; their brains knocked out; children two or three months old; all ages lying there, from sucking infants up to warriors.

I do not think that I saw more than 70 lying dead then, as far as I went.

JAMES D. CANNON, FIRST LIEUTENANT
First Infantry New Mexico Volunteers

The Chivington Massacre, Affidavit, January 16, 1865, p. 53—The command of Colonel Chivington was composed of about one thousand men; the village of the Indians consisted of from one hundred to one hundred and thirty lodges, and, as far as I am able to judge, of from five hundred to six hundred souls, the majority of which were women and children; in going over the battle-ground the next day I did not see a body of man, woman, or child but was scalped, and in many instances their bodies were mutilated in the most horrible manner—men, women, and children's privates cut out, &c; I heard one man say that he had cut out a woman's private parts and had them for exhibition on a stick; I heard another man say that he had cut the fingers off an Indian to get the rings on the hand; according to the best of my knowledge and belief these atrocities that were committed were with knowledge of J. M. Chivington, and I do not know of his taking any measures to prevent them; I heard of one instance of a child a few months old being thrown in the feed-box of a wagon, and after being carried some distance left on the ground to perish; I also heard of numerous instances in which men had cut out the private parts of females and stretched them over the saddle-bows, and wore them over their hats while riding in the ranks. All these matters were a subject of general conversation, and could not help being known by Colonel J. M. Chivington.

Sand Creek Massacre, Testimony, p. 111—My estimate of the number of Indians killed was about two hundred, all told.

They were scalped and mutilated in various ways.

p. 113—I heard one man say that he had cut a squaw's heart out, and he had it stuck up on a stick.

DAVID LOUDERBACK, PRIVATE
First Colorado Cavalry

The Chivington Massacre, Affidavit by Louderback and R. W. Clark, citizen, January 27, 1865, pp. 53–54— . . . that according to their best knowledge and belief the entire Indian village was composed of not more than five hundred (500) souls, two-thirds of which were women and children; that the dead bodies of women and children were afterwards mutilated in the most horrible manner; that it was the understanding of the deponents, and the general understanding of the garrison of Fort Lyon, that this village were friendly Indians. . . .

Sand Creek Massacre, Testimony, p. 137—(How many Indians were killed?) That I cannot say, as I did not go up above to count them. I saw only eight. I could not stand it; they were cut up too much. . . . they were scalped and cut up in an awful manner; what I saw were.

p. 138—White Antelope was killed in the bed of the creek and Standing-in-the-Water was killed right opposite to him, on the left hand side of the creek. After they were killed they were scalped, and White Antelope's nose, ears, and privates were cut off. . . .

The pappoose was carried in a feed-box of a wagon a day or a day and a half, and then it was thrown out and left in the road; I do not know whether they killed it or not.

p. 141—Men and officers of the command told me it was thrown out. . . .

The Arapahoe squaw that came in here after the command had left for Denver stated to John Smith that she had found the child on the road and cut its throat.

W. P. MINTON, SECOND LIEUTENANT
First New Mexico Volunteers
and
C. M. COSSITT, FIRST LIEUTENANT
First Cavalry of Colorado

The Chivington Massacre, Affidavit, January 27, 1865, p. 54— . . . according to representations made by others in our presence, murdered their women and children, and committed the most horrible outrages upon the dead bodies of the same. . . .

JAMES OLNEY, FIRST LIEUTENANT
First Colorado Cavalry

The Chivington Massacre, Affidavit, April 20, 1865, p. 61—

That he was present at the massacre of the Indians at Sand Creek by Colonel Chivington, on the twenty-ninth day of November, 1864; that during that massacre he saw three squaws and five children, prisoners in charge of some soldiers; that, while they were being conducted along, they were approached by Lieutenant Harry Richmond, of the third Colorado cavalry; that Lieutenant Richmond thereupon immediately killed and scalped the three women and the five children while they (the prisoners) were screaming for mercy; while the soldiers in whose charge these prisoners were shrank back, apparently aghast.

E. W. WYNKOOP, MAJOR
First Colorado Cavalry

The Chivington Massacre, Report, January 16, 1865, p. 63— Numerous eye-witnesses have described scenes to me, coming under the notice of Colonel Chivington, of the most disgusting and horrible character, the dead bodies of females profaned in such a manner that the recital is sickening. . . . I have been informed by Captain Booth, district inspector, that he visited the field and counted but sixty-nine bodies, and by others who were present, but that few, if any, over that number were killed, and that two-thirds of them were women and children.

L. WILSON, CAPTAIN
First Colorado Cavalry

The Chivington Massacre, Affidavit, p. 67—The squaws and pappooses followed the column to Fort Lyon; one young infant was picked up on the field; when we got into camp it was given to one of the squaws, but afterwards died and was buried. I saw some Indians that had been scalped, and the ears were cut off of the body of White Antelope. One Indian who had been scalped had also his skull all smashed in, and I heard that the privates of White Antelope had been cut off to make a tobacco bag out of. I heard some of the men say that the privates of one of the squaws had been cut out and put on a stick.

PRESLEY TALBOTT, FORMERLY CAPTAIN
Third Regiment Colorado Cavalry

The Chivington Massacre, Affidavit, p. 68—I did not see any flags displayed by the Indians.

JACOB DOWNING, FORMERLY MAJOR
First Colorado Cavalry

The Chivington Massacre, Affidavit, July 21, 1865, pp. 68–70—My own belief is, that there were some five hundred or six hundred Indians killed; I counted two hundred and odd Indians within a very short distance or where their village stood, most of whom were in these trenches, and Indians were killed five and six miles from the village; but of the two hundred killed, I counted about twelve or fifteen women and a few children, who had been killed in the trenches. I did not see any flag over the village, but afterwards saw a man with a small flag, who said he got it out of a lodge. . . . I saw no soldier scalping anybody, but saw one or two bodies which evidently had been scalped. . . . I saw no mutilated bodies besides scalping, but heard that some bodies were mutilated. I don't know that I saw any squaw that had been scalped. I saw no scalps or other parts of the person among the command on our return. I saw no papoose in a feed-box. I think I saw one with a squaw the night of our first camp, but understood they abandoned it the next morning when the command moved.

DR. CALEB S. BURDSAL, FORMERLY ASSISTANT SURGEON
Third Regiment Colorado Cavalry

The Chivington Massacre, Affidavit, p. 72— . . . a soldier came to the opening of the lodge and called my attention to

183

some white scalps he held in his hand; my impression, after examination, was that two or three of them were quite fresh; I saw in the hands of soldiers silk dresses and other garments belonging to women; I saw some squaws that were dead, but did not go over the ground; I did not see any Indian scalped, but saw the bodies after they were scalped; I saw no other mutilations; I did not see any kind of a flag in the Indian camp; there were none left wounded on the field; I know of none being killed after being taken prisoner. . . . I think Colonel Chivington was in a position where he must have seen the scalping going on.

Sand Creek Massacre, Testimony, p. 203— . . . I was in the lodge dressing the wounded; some man came to the opening of the lodge and hallooed to me to look at five or six scalps he had in his hand. I should judge, from a casual look, that they were the scalps of white persons.

p. 204—My impression is that one or two of them were not more than ten days off the head.

ASBURY BIRD, SOLDIER
Co. D, First Colorado Cavalry

The Chivington Massacre, Affidavit, p. 72—I went over the ground soon after the battle. I should judge there were between 400 and 500 Indians killed. I counted 350 lying up and down the creek. I think about half the killed were women and children. Nearly all, men, women, and children, were scalped. I saw one woman whose privates had been mutilated. The scalps were carried away mostly by the 3d regiment, one-hundred-day men. I saw but one Indian infant killed.

JOSEPH A. CRAMER, SECOND LIEUTENANT
First Colorado Cavalry

The Chivington Massacre, Affidavit, p. 73—I estimated the loss of the Indians to be from one hundred and twenty-five to one hundred and seventy-five killed; no wounded fell into our hands, and all the dead were scalped. The Indian who was pointed out as White Antelope had his fingers cut off. . . . It is a mistake that there were any white scalps found in the village. I saw one, but it was very old, the hair being much faded. I was ordered to burn the village, and was through all the lodges. There was not any snow on the ground, and no rifle-pits.

Sand Creek Massacre, Testimony, p. 50—I estimated them [the dead Indians] at one hundred and seventy-five or one hundred and eighty. . . . I do not recollect seeing one but what was scalped. . . . I did not see any rifle-pits.

p. 51—There was one little child but a few months old, brought one day's march from Sand creek and then abandoned; so I was told by enlisted men of the command.

LUCIEN PALMER, SERGEANT
Co. C, First Colorado Cavalry

The Chivington Massacre, Affidavit, p. 74—I counted 130 bodies, all dead; two squaws and three papooses were captured and brought to Fort Lyon. I think among the dead bodies one-third were women and children. The bodies were horribly cut up, skulls broken in a good many; I judge they were broken in after they were killed, as they were shot besides. I do not think I saw any but what was scalped; saw fingers cut off, saw several bodies with privates cut off, women as well as men. I saw Major Sayre, of the 3d regiment, scalp an Indian for the scalp lock ornamented by silver ornaments; he cut off the skin with it. He stood by and saw his men cutting fingers from dead bodies . . . . All I saw done in mutilating bodies was done by members of the 3d regiment.

Sand Creek Massacre, Testimony, p. 143— . . . the other pappoose was left at our first camp this side of Sand Creek. . . . They [the dead Indians] were scalped; skulls broken in in several instances; I saw several of the third regiment cut off their fingers to get the rings off of them; I saw Major Sayre scalp

185

a dead Indian; the scalp had a long tail of silver hanging to it. . . .

AMOS C. MIKSCH, CORPORAL
Co. E, First Colorado Cavalry

The Chivington Massacre, Affidavit, pp. 74–75—Next morning after the battle I saw a little boy covered up among the Indians in a trench, still alive. I saw a major in the 3d regiment take out his pistol and blow off the top of his head. I saw some men unjointing fingers to get rings off, and cutting off ears to get silver ornaments. I saw a party with the same major take up bodies that had been buried in the night to scalp them and take off ornaments. I saw a squaw with her head smashed in before she was killed. Next morning, after they were dead and stiff, these men pulled out the bodies of the squaws and pulled them open in an indecent manner. I heard men say they had cut out the privates, but did not see it myself. It was the 3d Colorado men who did these things. I counted 123 dead bodies; I think not over twenty-five were full-grown men; the warriors were killed out in the bluff. . . . Next day I saw Lieutenant Richmond scalp two Indians; it was disgusting to me; I heard nothing of a fresh white scalp in the Indian camp until I saw it in the Dunn papers. There was no snow on the ground; there were no rifle-pits except what the Indians dug into the sand-bank after we commenced firing.

JOHN M. CHIVINGTON, FORMERLY COLONEL
First Colorado Cavalry

The Chivington Massacre, Report, November 29, 1864, p. 91—We killed chiefs Black Kettle, White Antelope, and Little Robe, and between four and five hundred other Indians; captured between four and five hundred ponies and mules. . . . We found a white man's scalp, not more than three days old, in a lodge.

Massacre of Cheyenne Indians, Report, December 16, 1864,

p. 49—Between five and six hundred Indians were left dead upon the field. . . . I was shown the scalp of a white man, found in one of the lodges, which could not have been taken more than two or three days previous.

p. 102—Testimony—There was an unusual number of males among them [the Indians at Sand Creek], for the reason that the war chiefs of both nations were assembled there evidently for some special purpose. . . . They [trenches] were found at various points extending along the banks of the creek for several miles from the camp; there were marks of the pick and shovel used in excavating them. . . . From the best information I could obtain, I judge there were five hundred or six hundred Indians killed. . . .

p. 103—I myself passed over some portions of the field after the fight, and I saw but one woman who had been killed, and one who had hanged herself; I saw no dead children. From all I could learn, I arrived at the conclusion that but few women or children had been slain.

p. 108—On my arrival at Fort Lyon, in all my conversations with Major Anthony commanding the post, and Major Colley, Indian agent, I heard nothing of this recent statement that the Indians were under the protection of the government &c. . . .

Scott J. Anthony, formerly Major
First Colorado Cavalry

Massacre of Cheyenne Indians, Testimony, p. 17— The loss on our side was 49 men killed and wounded; on theirs I suppose it was about 125.

p. 22—At one time I sent out a scouting party and told them to look over the ground. They came back and reported to me that they had counted 69 dead bodies there. About two-thirds of those were women and children.

p. 26—I saw one man dismount from his horse; he was standing by the side of Colonel Chivington. There was a dead squaw there who had apparently been killed some little time before. The man got down off his horse, took hold of the squaw, took out his knife and tried to cut off her scalp. I thought the squaw had been scalped before; a spot on the side of the head had evidently been cut off before with a knife. . . . I saw a great many Indians and squaws that had been scalped. . . . I heard a report some twenty days after the fight—I saw a notice in Colonel Chivington's report—that a scalp three days old, a white woman's scalp, was found in the Cheyenne camp. I did not hear anything about that until after Colonel Chivington had reached Denver. I was with him for ten days after the fight, and never heard a word about a white woman's scalp being found in camp until afterwards. . . .

. . . he [Anthony's adjutant] speaks in his affidavit about the bodies of the Indians having been so badly mutilated, their privates cut off, and all that kind of thing. I never saw anything of that. . . . Yet it was a matter of daily conversation between us at the post. I, however, did myself see some bodies that were mutilated.

p. 27—There was one little child, probably three years old, just big enough to walk through the sand. The Indians had gone ahead, and this little child was behind following after them. The little fellow was perfectly naked, travelling on the sand. I saw one man get off his horse, at a distance of about seventy-five yards, and draw up his rifle and fire—he missed the child. Another man came up and said, "Let me try the son of a bitch; I can hit him." He got down off his horse, kneeled down and fired at the little child, but he missed him. A third man came up and made a similar remark, and fired, and the little fellow dropped.

LEAVITT BOWEN, FORMERLY LT. COLONEL
Third Regiment Colorado Cavalry

Massacre of Cheyenne Indians, Report, November 30, 1864, p. 52—From the most reliable information, from actual count and positions occupied, I have no doubt that at least one hundred and fifty Indians were killed by my battalion.

The war flag of this band of Cheyennes is in my possession, presented by Stephen Decatur, commissary sergeant of company C, who acted as my battalion adjutant.

SILAS S. SOULE, CAPTAIN
First Colorado Cavalry

Sand Creek Massacre, Testimony, p. 11—I went to Sand Creek on the last of December with about thirty men, accompanied by Captain Booth, inspecting officer and chief of cavalry, district of the upper Arkansas. Saw sixty-nine dead Indians and about one hundred live dogs, and two live ponies and a few dead ones.

p. 23—They [Indian children] were scalped I know; I saw holes in them, and some with their skulls knocked in, but cannot say how they were mutilated.

. . . I saw soldiers with children's scalps during the day, but did not see them cut them off.

JAMES P. BECKWITH, FRONTIERSMAN

Sand Creek Massacre, Testimony, p. 69—It is impossible for me to say how many were killed. A great many were killed, but I cannot guess within a hundred how many were killed.

p. 70—About two-thirds [were women and children] . . .

(Was White Antelope scalped and otherwise mutilated?) Yes, both.

p. 71—. . . I saw several men scalping, but I know not their names; but there is only one man that I know who scalped an Indian I killed myself.

. . . I only saw White Antelope that had been mutilated otherwise than by scalping.

N. D. SNYDER, SOLDIER
Co. D, First Colorado Cavalry

Sand Creek Massacre, Testimony, p. 77—(Did you see an American flag?) Yes, at the lower end of the village. The west end . . . I saw ninety-eight [dead Indians on visit to battle-ground with Soule and Boothe after the fight] . . . the boys in the third regiment [did the scalping]; also the boys in the first regiment.

GEORGE M. ROAN, SOLDIER
Co. C, First Colorado Cavalry

Sand Creek Massacre, Testimony, p. 142—I saw a camp of Indians, and the stars and stripes waving over the camp.

AMOS D. JAMES, SOLDIER
Co. C, First Colorado Cavalry

Sand Creek Massacre, Testimony, p. 145—The morning we left the battleground I rode over the field; I saw in riding over the field a man (a sergeant of the 3d) dismount from his horse and cut the ear from the body of an Indian, and the scalp from the head of another. I saw a number of children killed; I suppose they were shot, they had bullet holes in them; one child had been cut with some instrument across the side. I saw another that both ears had been cut off. . . . I cannot say how many [dead Indians] I saw; I did not count all; I counted one hundred or a little over.

JAMES J. ADAMS, CORPORAL
Co. C, First Colorado Cavalry

Sand Creek Massacre, Testimony, p. 150—I did not see any [dead Indians] but what were scalped. . . . There was one person [engaged in scalping] that they called Major. There was another officer there. . . they called Richmond. . . . There were some privates engaged in scalping, likewise, in the same party. I saw some men cutting the fingers off of dead Indians to get the rings off.

GEORGE L. SHOUP, FORMERLY COLONEL
Third Regiment Colorado Cavalry

Sand Creek Massacre, Deposition, p. 176—From my own observation I should say [there were] about three hundred [Indians killed].

p. 177—I saw one or two men who were in the act of scalping, but I am not positive.

ANDREW J. GILL, CAPTAIN
Territorial Militia

Sand Creek Massacre, Affidavit, p. 180—I saw one soldier scalp an Indian.

STEPHEN DECATUR, FORMERLY SERGEANT
Third Regiment Colorado Cavalry

Sand Creek Massacre, Testimony, p. 195—The next day after the battle I went over the battle-ground, in the capacity of clerk, for Lieutenant Colonel Bowen, and counted four hundred and fifty dead Indian warriors. . . . As I was going out to get some of the lodge-poles for wood, I saw some of the men opening bundles or bales. I saw them take therefrom a number of white persons' scalps—men's, women's, and children's; some daguerreotypes, ladies' wearing apparel and white children's, and saw part of a lady's toilet and one box of rouge, also a box containing a powder puff. I saw one scalp of a white woman in particular. . . . I saw, comparatively speaking, a small number of women killed.

p. 199—There were a great many of them [rifle pits], I did not count the number; they were deep enough for men to lie down and conceal themselves, and load their guns in; some of them I should think deeper than three feet.

THADDEUS P. BELL, SOLDIER

Sand Creek Massacre, Testimony, p. 223—I saw a good

many white scalps there [at Sand Creek]. The number, I have not any idea how many. There were some that looked old, as if they might have been taken a considerable time; others not so long, and one that was quite fresh, not over from five to eight days old at furthest. . . . The fresh scalp was from a red haired man.

ROBERT BENT, GUIDE

The Chivington Massacre, Sworn Statement, pp. 95–96— When we came in sight of the camp I saw the American flag waving and heard Black Kettle tell the Indians to stand round the flag, and there they were huddled—men, women, and children. This was when we were within fifty yards of the Indians. I also saw a white flag raised. These flags were in so conspicuous a position that they must have been seen. When the troops fired the Indians ran, some of the men ran into their lodges, probably to get their arms. They had time to get away if they had wanted to. . . . I think there were six hundred Indians in all. I think there were thirty-five braves and some old men, about sixty in all. All fought well. At the time the rest of the men were away from camp, hunting. I visited the battleground one month afterwards; saw the remains of a good many; counted sixty-nine, but a number had been eaten by the wolves and dogs. . . . Everyone I saw dead was scalped.

BIBLIOGRAPHY

Manuscripts

Bent, George. "Letters to George E. Hyde," MS XXI, Colorado State Historical Society, Denver, Colorado.

———. "Three Letters to Colonel Tappan," Feb. 23, 1889; March 15, 1889; April 16, 1889. Copies in Colorado State Historical Society, Denver, Colorado.

Chivington, Colonel J. M. "The First Colorado Regiment," Denver, Colorado, October 18, 1884. Colorado State Historical Society, Denver, Colorado.

"Dawson Scrapbooks." Colorado State Historical Society, Denver, Colorado.

Stuart, J. E. B. "Diary." Microfilm, Kansas State Historical Society, Topeka, Kansas.

Tappan, Samuel F. "Unpublished Autobiography," March 12, 1895. Kansas State Historical Society, Topeka, Kansas.

———. "Diary." Microfilm, Colorado State Historical Society, Denver, Colorado.

Wynkoop, Edward W. "Wynkoop's Unfinished Manuscript." Colorado State Historical Society, Denver, Colorado.

GOVERNMENT DOCUMENTS

Congressional Globe, 38 Cong., 2 sess. Washington, Office of John C. Rives, 1865.

United States Congress, House of Representatives. "Massacre of Cheyenne Indians," *Report on the Conduct of the War*, 38 Cong., 2 sess. Washington, G. P. O., 1865.

———, Senate. "Sand Creek Massacre," *Report of the Secretary of War, Sen. Exec. Doc. 26*, 39 Cong., 2 sess. Washington, G. P. O., 1867.

———, ———. "The Chivington Massacre," *Reports of the Committees*, 39 Cong., 2 sess. Washington, G. P. O., 1867.

———, ———. *Indian Affairs, Laws and Treaties.* Vol. II. *Sen. Exec. Doc. 319*, 58 Cong., 2 sess. Edited by C. J. Kappler. Washington, G. P. O., 1904.

United States Interior Department, Bureau of Indian Affairs. *Reports of the Commissioner of Indian Affairs for the Years 1851 through 1865* (in separate volumes for each year). Washington, G. P. O., 1852–66.

United States War Department. *The War of the Rebellion. A Compilation of the Official Records of the Union and Confederate Armies.* Four series, 128 vols. Washington, G. P. O., 1880–1901.

NEWSPAPERS

Commonwealth Weekly, Denver, June 15, 1864; June 22, 1864.

Daily National Intelligencer, Washington, D. C., March 28, 1863.

Daily Times, Leavenworth, Kansas, Sept. 27, 1860; Oct. 9, 1860; Oct. 23, 1860.

Denver Republican, July 15, 1884; April 20 to May 18, 1890.

Evening Star, Washington, D. C., March 3, 1863; March 27, 1863.

National Republican, Washington, D. C., March 27, 1863.
Rocky Mountain Herald, Denver, August 24, 1861.
Rocky Mountain News (Daily), Denver, 1861–65.
Rocky Mountain News (Weekly), Denver, 1864.
Washington Daily Morning Chronicle, May 4, 1863; May 29, 1863.
Western Mountaineer, Golden, Sept. 20, 1860; Oct. 4, 1860.

Books

Baker, James B., ed., and LeRoy R. Hafen, associate ed. *History of Colorado*. Vol. I. Denver, Linderman Co., Inc., 1927.

Beardsley, Isaac Haight. *Echoes from Peak and Plain, or Tales of Life, War, Travel, and Colorado Methodism*. Cincinnati, Curtis and Jennings; New York, Eaton and Mains, 1890.

Blackman, Frank W., ed. *Kansas—A Cyclopedia of State History, Embracing Events, Institutions, Industries, Counties, Cities, Towns, Prominent Persons, etc.* Cincinnati, Standard Publishing Co., 1912.

Breakenridge, William M. *Helldorado, Bringing the Law to the Mesquite*. Boston and New York, Houghton Mifflin Co., 1928.

Craig, Reginald S. *The Fighting Parson, the Biography of Colonel John M. Chivington*. Los Angeles, Westernlore Press, 1959.

Dunn, James P., Jr. *Massacre of the Mountains*. New York, Harper and Brothers, 1886.

Gardiner, Dorothy. *The Great Betrayal*. Garden City, New York, Doubleday and Co., Inc., 1949.

Garrard, Lewis H. *Wah-to-yah and the Taos Trail*. Edited by Ralph P. Bieber. Glendale, California, Arthur H. Clark Company, 1938.

Grinnell, George Bird. *The Fighting Cheyennes*. Norman, University of Oklahoma Press, 1956.

———. *The Cheyenne Indians*. New Haven, Conn., Yale University Press, 1923.

Hafen, LeRoy R., and Francis Marion Young, eds. *Fort Laramie and the Pageant of the West, 1834–1890*. Glendale, Calif., Arthur H. Clark Company, 1938.

Hafen, LeRoy R., ed. *Pike's Peak Gold Rush Guidebooks of 1859*,

Southwest Historical Series, Vol. IX. Glendale, Calif., Arthur H. Clark Company, 1941.

———, ed. *Colorado Gold Rush,* Southwest Historical Series, Vol. X. Glendale, Calif., Arthur H. Clark Company, 1941.

———, ed. *Colorado and Its People.* Vol. I. New York, Lewis Historical Publishing Co., Inc., 1948.

Hall, Frank. *History of the State of Colorado.* Chicago, The Blakely Printing Co., 1889.

Hill, Alice Polk. *Tales of the Colorado Pioneers.* Denver, Pierson and Gardiner, 1884.

Hollister, Ovando J. *Boldly They Rode: A History of the First Colorado Regiment of Volunteers.* Lakewood, Colorado, The Golden Press, 1949. (Original edition published in 1863 entitled *A History of the First Regiment of Colorado Volunteers.*)

Howbert, Irving. *Memories of a Lifetime in the Pike's Peak Region.* New York, G. P. Putnam's Sons, 1925.

———. *The Indians of the Pike's Peak Region.* New York, Knickerbocker Press, 1914.

Inman, Colonel Henry. *The Old Santa Fe Trail. The Story of a Great Highway.* New York, The Macmillan Co., 1897.

Jablow, Joseph. *The Cheyenne in Plains Indian Trade Relations, 1795–1840.* New York, J. J. Augustin, Inc., 1951.

Jackson, Helen Hunt. *A Century of Dishonor.* Boston, Roberts Brothers, 1887.

Lavender, David. *Bent's Fort.* Garden City, New York, Doubleday and Co., Inc., 1954.

McMechen, Edgar Carlisle. *Life of Governor Evans.* Denver, The Walgren Publishing Co., 1924.

Mumey, Nolie. *History of the Early Settlements of Denver (1859–1860).* Glendale, Calif., Arthur H. Clark Company, 1942.

Pitzer, Henry Littleton. *Three Frontiers. Memories and a portrait of Henry Littleton Pitzer as recorded by his son Robert Claiborne Pitzer.* Muscatine, Iowa, The Prairie Press, 1938.

Ryus, William H. *The Second William Penn. Treating with the Indians on the Santa Fe Trail, 1860–66.* Kansas City, Missouri, Frank T. Riley Publishing Co., 1913.

Sabin, Edwin L. *Kit Carson Days*. Vol. II. New York, The Press of the Pioneers, 1935.

Stoeckel, Carl, and Ellen Battelle. *Correspondence of John Sedgwick Major General*. New York, The DeVinne Press, 1903.

Thayer, William M. *Marvels of the New West*. Norwich, Conn., The Henry Bill Publishing Company, 1888.

Ware, Captain Eugene F. *The Indian War of 1864*, Introduction by Clyde C. Walton. New York, St. Martin's Press, 1960.

Whitford, William Clarke. *Colorado Volunteers in the Civil War. The New Mexico Campaign in 1862*. Denver, The State Historical and Natural History Society, 1906.

Williams, Mrs. Ellen. *Three Years and a Half in the Army: or History of the Second Colorados*. New York, Fowler and Wells Co., 1885.

Willison, George F. *Here They Dug the Gold*. New York, Brentano's, Inc., 1931.

Zornow, William Frank. *Kansas: A History of the Jayhawk State*. Norman, University of Oklahoma Press, 1957.

ARTICLES

Adams, Blanche V. "The Second Colorado Cavalry in the Civil War," *The Colorado Magazine*, Vol. VIII (May, 1931).

Ashley, Susan Riley. "Reminiscences of Colorado in the Early 'Sixties," *The Colorado Magazine*, Vol. XIII (November, 1936).

Blunt, James G. "General Blunt's Account of His Civil War Experiences," *The Kansas Historical Quarterly*, Vol. I (1932).

Chivington, J. M. "The Pet Lambs," *Denver Republican* (April 20, 1890 through May 18, 1890).

Dawson, Thomas F. "Colonel Boone's Treaty with the Plains Indians," *The Trail*, Vol. XIV (July, 1921).

Dormis, John T., ed. "The Chivingtons" *The Masonic News-Digest*, Vol. XXXIV (June 28, 1957).

Ellis, Elmer. "Colorado's First Fight for Statehood, 1865–1868," *The Colorado Magazine*, Vol. VIII (January, 1931).

Englert, Kenneth E. "Raids by Reynolds," *1956 Brand Book of The*

Denver Westerners. Boulder, Colorado, Johnson Publishing Co., 1957.

Foreman, Carolyn Thomas. "Col. Jesse Henry Leavenworth," *Chronicles of Oklahoma,* Vol. XIII (1935).

Flynn, A. J. "Creating a Commonwealth," *The Colorado Magazine,* Vol. I (July, 1924).

Grinnell, George Bird. "Bent's Old Fort and Its Builders." Reprint from a chapter in *Beyond the Old Frontier.* New York, Charles Scribner's Sons, 1913.

Hafen, LeRoy R., ed. "The Last Years of James P. Beckwourth," *The Colorado Magazine,* Vol. V (August, 1928).

———. "The W. M. Boggs Manuscript About Bent's Fort, Kit Carson, the Far West and Life Among the Indians," *The Colorado Magazine,* Vol. VII (March, 1930).

Harvey, James R., interview with Elizabeth J. Tallman. "Pioneer Experiences in Colorado," *The Colorado Magazine,* Vol. XIII (July, 1936).

Hill, Nathaniel. "Nathaniel Hill Inspects Colorado, Letters Written in 1864," *The Colorado Magazine,* Vol. XXXIV (January, 1957).

Hundall, Mary Prowers. "Early History of Bent County," *The Colorado Magazine,* Vol. XXII (November, 1945).

Lambert, Julia S. "Plain Tales of the Plains," *The Trail,* Vol. VII (January-September, 1916).

Lecompte, Janet. "Charles Autobees," *The Colorado Magazine,* Vol. XXXVI (July, 1959).

Lubers, H. L. "William Bent's Family and the Indians of the Plains," *The Colorado Magazine,* Vol. XIII (January, 1936).

Morse, O. E. "An Attempted Rescue of John Brown from Charlestown, Va., Jail." Kansas State Historical Society, Vol. VIII (1903-1904).

Mumey, Dr. Nolie. "John Milton Chivington, the Misunderstood Man," *1956 Brand Book of the Denver Westerners.* Boulder, Colorado, Johnson Publishing Co., 1957.

Perrigo, Lynn I. "Major Hal Sayre's Diary of the Sand Creek Campaign," *The Colorado Magazine,* Vol. XIV (July, 1921).

Prentice, C. A. "Captain Silas S. Soule, a Pioneer Martyr," *The Colorado Magazine*, Vol. IV (May, 1927).

Root, George A. "Extracts from Diary of Captain Lambert Wolf," *The Kansas State Historical Quarterly*, Vol. I (1931–32).

Sanford, Albert B. "The Big Flood in Cherry Creek, 1864," *The Colorado Magazine*, Vol. IV (May, 1927).

———, ed. "Life at Camp Weld and Fort Lyon in 1861–62. An Extract from the Diary of Mrs. Byron N. Sanford," *The Colorado Magazine*, Vol. VII (May, 1930).

INDEX

with chiefs, 121; sent to reassure Indians, 126; goes to Sand Creek, 128, 148; at massacre, 149, 152–53, 155; testifies concerning massacre, 165, 168; at Medicine Lodge, 174; dies, 175; testimony on massacre, 178–79

Smith, John W. (scout): 16 n., 52 n.

Smoky Hill River: 31, 32, 33, 41, 50, 51, 52 n., 76, 99, 109, 123, 126, 128, 133, 141, 142, 154, 155, 160, 178; Cheyennes congregated on, 98; Wynkoop's expedition to, 97 n., 100–107, 110

Soule, Captain Silas S.: 27, 85, 88, 122, 138, 139, 155 n., 159, 170, 171 n., 173, 175, 190; at Smoky Hill 101; takes pledge, 102 n.; attends Camp Weld council, 111, 113; photograph made with chiefs, 120; biographical sketch, 138 n.; meets Chivington near Fort Lyon, 140; opposes Chivington, 141–42; threatened by Chivington, 142; commands Company D at massacre, 144; at massacre, 147; refuses to order troops to fire, 151; escorts train back to Fort Lyon, 153; conduct of reported by Chivington, 161; marries, 171; killed by Squiers, 172; testimony on massacre, 189

South Park, Colorado: 65, 66

South Platte River: 5, 15 n., 23, 37, 38, 43 n., 44, 46, 47, 48, 131, 133, 136, 147

Spotted Crow, Cheyenne chief, listed as killed: 154 n.

Spotted Horse, Cheyenne-Sioux Indian: 38 n., 42 n.

Spring Bottom, Colorado: 137, 144 n.

Squiers (soldier), kills Soule: 172

Standing-in-the-Water, Cheyenne chief: 181; visits Washington, D. C., 25; listed as killed, 154 n.

Stanton, Secretary of War: 60, 68, 69, 70, 132, 134

Starr carbines: 134; fail to fire, 87

Steck, Amos, attends Camp Weld council: 113

Stilwell, Lieutenant George H.: 55; on commission investigating massacre, 170

Storm, Arapaho chief: given medal, 11; signs treaty of Fort Wise, 16

Stuart, Lieutenant J. E. B., at Fort Wise: 9 n.

Sumner, General E. V.: 5, 28, 108 n.

Talbot, Captain Presley: commands Company M, 131 n.; testifies concerning massacre, 173; affidavit on massacre, 183

Tall Bear, Cheyenne chief, signs treaty of Fort Wise, 16

UNIVERSITY OF OKLAHOMA PRESS : NORMAN